Conversations with God

A CATHOLIC VIEW OF PROPHECY

Robert Baldwin

Our Sunday Visitor Publishing Division
Our Sunday Visitor, Inc.
Huntington, Indiana 46750

Acknowledgments: Scripture excerpts in this work are quoted verbatim from or otherwise based on the *New American Bible*, © 1970 by the Confraternity of Christian Doctrine, Washington, D.C., and the *Revised Standard Version Bible, Catholic Edition,* © 1965 and 1966 by the Division of Christian Education of the National Council of the Churches of Christ in the U.S.A., and used by permission of the copyright owners, all rights reserved. Other sources from which material has been excerpted or has served as the basis for portions of this book are cited in the bibliography. The author is grateful to the copyright owners for the use of their materials. If any copyrighted materials have been inadvertently used in this work without proper credit being given, please notify Our Sunday Visitor in writing so that future printings of this work may be corrected accordingly.

Our Sunday Visitor Publishing Division
Our Sunday Visitor, Inc.
200 Noll Plaza
Huntington, Indiana 46750

International Standard Book Number: 0-87973-517-1
Library of Congress Catalog Card Number: 87-61382

Cover design by Steve A. Windmiller

PRINTED IN THE UNITED STATES OF AMERICA

To Sarah, Holly, and Elizabeth

CONTENTS

PREFACE

Until the flowering of the Second Vatican Council and the charismatic renewal, it had never occurred to me that there might be prophets among us in the modern church. I had assumed that prophets were people who belonged to a bygone era.

I knew that once upon a time God had spoken to the Jews through men like Moses, Amos, and Isaiah, and I knew that in the early church the "gift of prophecy" had been a sign of the Holy Spirit's presence. But I had assumed that in the modern church God had more or less abandoned such means of communication.

Sure, an occasional saint might be granted prophetic visions and revelations, but these were extraordinary experiences, not shared by any of the Catholics I knew. To me, God's word had become a static thing, spoken in biblical times, preserved in the Bible, and interpreted over the centuries by the hierarchy of the church.

In those days, I was not yet a Catholic because I had not discovered the living presence of Christ in the church. I was not alone. In the 1960s, some theologians were claiming that God was dead.

But a decade after Pope John XXIII had convened the Second Vatican Council with a prayer for "a new Pentecost," I was astounded to discover Catholic priests, religious, and lay people speaking what they believed to be messages from God. In charismatic prayer groups around the world, Catholics and other Christians were claiming they had found an intimate relationship with a loving God who conversed with them.

One of the bumper stickers of the day declared, "My God isn't dead. I spoke to him this morning. Sorry about yours." If what the charismatics were saying was true, God was not only listening to his people but was also speaking to them.

As I listened to the prophecies at charismatic prayer meetings I realized that God's love for me was more than I could fathom: that he had become a man and had willingly tasted death on a cross so that I might be saved. It was through charismatic preaching and prophecy that this Good News finally penetrated my thirty-seven-year-old heart and I became a Catholic.

Yet I couldn't help wondering why the rest of the church had so little to say about what was happening among the charismatics. I was aware of a few isolated attempts by bishops to keep the movement out of their dioceses and also aware of other bishops who welcomed it, but in the early days of the Catholic charismatic renewal, most of the hierarchy seemed to be following a "wait and see" policy.

When I was preparing for baptism, I once asked a

charismatic priest what the pope's attitude was toward the charismatics and their prophecies. I was worried that the vicar of Christ might suppress the movement that had drawn me into the church.

The priest smiled and said, "If the Holy Father were to tell us to stop what we are doing, we would stop immediately." But Rome made no attempt to suppress it and, as the months and years went by, there were increasing signs of papal approval.

Still, I was bothered by a seeming contradiction: If charismatic prophecy was not authentic, wouldn't the church say so? And if it *was* authentic, if God *was* renewing the gift of prophecy in our own age, shouldn't the whole church, not just charismatics, be listening?

The research I did in writing this book has not fully resolved that contradiction for me, but it has given me a better understanding of what prophecy is and how it was understood in Old Testament times, the early church, and throughout Christian history.

I believe that God does, indeed, guide his church through the prophetic voices of individual believers. It is my hope that this book will help Catholics listen to those voices and grow in their ability to recognize the word of God.

— R.F.B.

CHAPTER ONE

Prophecy Then and Now

She was a perfectly ordinary-looking young woman and she spoke in a clear voice. Her words rolled out of the huge overhead speakers and filled every corner of the massive auditorium.

"Heed me, my friends," she said. "I am very much alive and walking among you and passing on my Father's words." An odd statement, but some thirteen thousand persons, most of them Catholics, hung on every word. Hundreds of clergy and religious were there — among them, sixteen bishops and a cardinal.

"I tell you, save

yourselves and your country while there is still time,"
the woman continued. "Take my banner, sound the call,
blow your trumpets, clash your cymbals, march across
your land proclaiming God as your savior — then, sooner
than you believe possible, yours again will be a glorious
land — again one nation under God."

Who was this ordinary-looking woman, and whose
banner was she talking about? Her own? She didn't look
like someone who would lead trumpeters and cymbalists
on cross-country marches. Yet the thousands of people
who filled the Providence, Rhode Island, Civic Center
that day seemed more inspired than confused by her
words. Most of them believed they were listening to a
prophet; that, somehow, this ordinary Catholic woman
was not speaking for herself but delivering a message
from God.

When she finished speaking, the assembly prayed
and rejoiced. No one, not even the bishops, expressed any
doubt that God, in the 1980s, would speak to a Catholic
assembly through a prophet.

Over the last two decades, the gift of prophecy has
become well-established among both Catholic and
Protestant charismatics. At prayer meetings throughout
the world, messages are spoken in the name of the Lord
every night of the week. It is not a gift that the average
Catholic churchgoer is likely to encounter at Sunday
Mass, but it has penetrated the walls of Saint Peter's
Basilica in Rome, the very capital of Roman
Catholicism.

On Pentecost Sunday in 1975, some twenty-five
thousand persons — including ten thousand charismatics

who were in Rome for the Third International
Conference of the Catholic Charismatic Renewal —
gathered together in the basilica to participate in a Mass
celebrated by Pope Paul VI.

Before the Mass was over, people were singing in
tongues and praising God with such unusual fervor that
Rome's *Daily American*, an English-language
newspaper, reported that "bishops, archbishops and
cardinals, struggling to keep their hats in place, sang and
danced in ecstasy, embracing one another and raising
their arms to heaven." What happened at that Mass
wasn't well received by everyone, though. Another
Roman newspaper referred to the same events as "a
mass illusion."

The next day, May 19, Cardinal Leo Josef Suenens
returned to the basilica to celebrate a Mass with the
visiting charismatics. The same fervent spirit was
present, and on this occasion at least two Americans
prophesied from the high altar. One of these declared,
"A time of darkness is coming on the world, but a time of
glory is coming for my people. I will pour out on you all
the gifts of the Spirit. I will prepare you for spiritual
combat; I will prepare you for a time of evangelism that
the world has never seen."

Pope Paul, who arrived at the close of the Mass,
warmly greeted the charismatics in French, Spanish,
and English, and seemed to encourage them in their
exercise of prophecy and other spiritual gifts. He called
for "all the spiritual gifts to be received with gratitude"
although, as Saint Paul had told the Corinthians nearly
twenty centuries earlier, the pope asked that even

greater emphasis be given to love because "the fruit of the Spirit is love."

The Holy Father wondered aloud if what was happening in the charismatic renewal was, in fact, an opportunity for renewal of the entire church and the world. "Why, in this case, do we not take every means to continue it?" he asked.

The pope's words did not constitute "official" approval of what the charismatics were doing, but they were a strong indication that exercise of such gifts of the Spirit as prophecy, healing, and speaking in tongues had again become acceptable, even desirable, within Catholic worship. I say "again" because what happened at Saint Peter's Basilica on Pentecost weekend in 1975 was not really new. Rather, it was a renewal of ancient church traditions and spiritual gifts that had all but disappeared from the Catholic church over the centuries.

The New Testament and other early Christian writings make it clear that during the first century, prophecy and other spiritual gifts were flourishing within the church. Paul, whose letters constitute most of the New Testament, frequently mentioned prophets and prophecy in the early church. He even devoted an entire discourse to the proper use of such spiritual gifts. The early church clearly established precedents for the exercise of spiritual gifts by its members. But how closely does the prophecy of today resemble the prophecy of the early church? Is it really the voice of God? Does God speak only to charismatics? If the charismatics are uttering true prophecy, why isn't the whole church listening? And if they are speaking false prophecy, why doesn't the church condemn it?

Those are all reasonable questions, but before we can answer them we need to examine the different forms that prophecy has taken in the past and the forms that it takes today.

Within the Old Testament, there is a clear difference between the prophets who appear in the early historical books and the classic prophetic writers like Isaiah who emerged centuries later. Among the earlier Hebrew prophets, there were persons who functioned more like seers and diviners than as revealers of God's word. To the Jews of their time, prophets were regarded as holy men who possessed supernatural powers that could be used for such purposes as delivering oracles and finding lost objects.

Isaiah, Jeremiah, Amos, and the other great authors of the late Old Testament period represent a more highly developed form of prophecy as the revelation of God's word. To the Jews of their time, prophecy often took the form of a message in which God admonished his chosen ones, called them to repentance, promised them peace and prosperity if they were faithful to him, and warned them of dire consequences that would come upon them if they were not.

In the early church, prophecy was seen as a gift of the Holy Spirit distributed among Christ's followers as a means of spreading the Gospel and strengthening the church as the Body of Christ. To Paul and other early Christians, prophecy was an important gift but one which might be given to any church member.

Most charismatics adhere to the New Testament

principle that prophecy is a gift of the Holy Spirit to be used for the building of the church. The Spirit distributes such gifts among Christians as he will, not as a sign of exceptional holiness but as a gift from God. Yet even among charismatics, the gift of prophecy can take many forms, depending on the personality of the prophet, the group to whom the prophecy is addressed, and the movement of the Holy Spirit.

In a small parish, prayer-group prophecy is frequently a simple expression of God's love. Often the setting is a church basement where perhaps two dozen persons sit in folding chairs arranged in a circle. The group sings, reads psalms, and prays spontaneously, saying things like, "Thank you for your faithfulness, Jesus"; "Father, we love you"; "Praise to you, Lord!"

Eventually, the spoken prayer fades away to a murmur, then silence. The people wait expectantly. Then someone begins to speak: "My people: I love you. Do not be afraid to open your hearts to me. You are precious to me."

Many prophecies are as simple as that. No foretelling of cataclysmic events. No warnings or threats. No magic. Just a simple message from God to his people: "I love you." Other prophecies, like the 1975 prophecies at Saint Peter's, are laden with promises of future glory and warnings of storms and danger.

Modern charismatic prophecies have certain elements in common. First, each prophecy contains a message spoken as if it came from God rather than the person who speaks it. When a charismatic prophecy contains the word "I," it doesn't refer to the prophet but to God.

Second, each prophecy is delivered as a revelation of God's word. In addition, it is timely. It is delivered as God's word to a particular group in a particular place and at a particular moment — not words that were revealed to Moses or John the Baptist thousands of years ago but words spoken directly to today's believers, now.

Moreover, each prophecy presents a view of God as Lord and creator of the universe. The validity of these prophecies is based on the belief that they are the word of the one, true God — a God whose truth and authority are supreme because he is who he is.

There is also a consistency in the messages contained in this type of prophecy. They express God's concern for his people, his faithfulness to their needs, and his desire for their salvation and fulfillment as members of Christ's Body, the church. There is a common misconception that prophecy is directed primarily toward predicting the future; but the gift of prophecy, as it is manifested among Catholic charismatics today, is directed more toward the expression of God's love and his concern for those he loves.

Modern prophecy, like biblical prophecy, sometimes includes promises of things to come — promises of the goodness that will follow when people listen to and obey God's word. But it rarely, if ever, makes specific predictions of events to come. That, in fact, is one of the striking differences between prophecy in the Judeo-Christian tradition and the so-called prophecies of ancient diviners or modern psychics and seers who make a living predicting earthquakes, airplane crashes, assassinations, and similar catastrophes to a gullible public.

In every age, there have been people who consulted soothsayers, diviners, oracles, fortune-tellers, spiritualists, ouija boards, and the like in an attempt to know the future or to make decisions. But the God who speaks in prophecy is not a God who can be employed by his creatures for such purposes. He speaks when he will, through whom he pleases; and we, if we are wise, will listen.

The verb "to prophesy," as it is used in the New Testament, means to "foretell" but not necessarily to predict the future. More often, prophecy will foretell the flowering of God's word without predicting specific events. The Old Testament prophet Isaiah, for instance, didn't prophesy specifically that in a certain year, Jesus of Nazareth would be born as the Messiah, would die on the cross to atone for the sins of mankind, and would then rise from the dead to bring new life to all who believed in him. Isaiah spoke in more general terms about the "Servant of the Lord" who gives his life as an offering for sin, and about the restoration of Israel. The prophecies of Isaiah, although they were fulfilled by Jesus, were not specific predictions but an assurance that God's love for his people would flower and bear fruit.

Father John L. McKenzie, the Catholic biblical scholar and author, makes this observation about the fulfillment of prophecy: "It is the fulfillment of a hope, a destiny, a plan, a reality."

The church sees the birth, ministry, death, and resurrection of Jesus as the fulfillment of many Old Testament prophecies. In a sense, he is the fulfillment of all prophecy.

Yet even after our Lord's resurrection and ascension, prophecy continued to be a normal feature of Christian worship for at least two centuries. After the second century, it began to decline. It didn't die out completely, but it became increasingly rare and was usually manifested in extraordinary persons known for their holiness.

From the Middle Ages until the twentieth century, prophecy was considered by many theologians to be a gift that functioned in the time of the apostles but which was no longer needed in the modern church. Along with the gifts of healing and speaking in tongues, it was considered to be an extraordinary gift that God had given to Christians for only a short season — to help establish the church. Once the church had gained a secure foothold in the Roman world, such gifts died out.

That view hasn't been entirely abandoned, but it has been challenged by the emergence in our own age of the charismatic renewal. If the charismatics are right, God is speaking to his people today through prophecy, just as he did in the time of Isaiah or in the church of the first century.

Prophecy and other long-dormant charismatic gifts began to noticeably reappear among some Protestant sects in the nineteenth century and among Catholic

worshipers in the late 1960s. In 1967, members of a
Catholic Bible study group at Duquesne University in
Pittsburgh reported they had experienced "baptism in
the Holy Spirit" and the reception of charismatic gifts,
including tongues and prophecy.

This occurred at a time when the Roman Catholic
Church was particularly open to change. The Second
Vatican Council had not only affirmed the need for such
openness but had seemed almost to portend a
charismatic renewal. Pope John XXIII, in convening the
council, petitioned God to "renew your wonders in our
time, as though for a new Pentecost." The council itself
paved the way for a fresh outpouring of the spiritual gifts
that had been manifested in the church at the time of
Pentecost. The council's *Dogmatic Constitution on
the Church* declares that "these charismatic gifts,
whether they be the most outstanding or the more simple
and widely diffused, are to be received with thanksgiving
and consolation for they are exceedingly suitable and
useful for the needs of the church."

That statement, adopted by the council in November,
1963, indicates a marked change from the idea that
charismatic gifts were a thing of the past. Less than four
years later, when the charismatic renewal erupted
within the Catholic Church, it based its legitimacy not
only on the historic precedents set by the early church
but also on the documents of Vatican II.

As a result, many Catholics who might otherwise
have been suspicious of the "new Pentecost" in their
midst, welcomed it. During the 1970s, charismatic
prayer groups burst forth like flowers in springtime. By

1985, there were an estimated seven and a half million Catholics throughout the world who considered themselves part of the charismatic movement.

Some bishops and cardinals have not only welcomed the renewal of spiritual gifts but have become actively involved in it. Their attitude is not unanimous, but, in general, the charismatic movement is welcomed and appreciated by the hierarchy. In essence, the church is telling its members to take God seriously, to be willing to hear his voice and to obey him.

This welcome is tempered by caution, however. Even as Vatican II was endorsing the validity of charismatic gifts, the council warned that "extraordinary gifts are not to be rashly sought after, nor are the fruits of apostolic labor to be presumptuously expected of them. In any case, judgment as to their authenticity and proper use belongs to those who preside over the church, and to whose special competence it belongs, not indeed to extinguish the Spirit, but to test all things and hold fast to that which is good."

Such caution is absolutely necessary and proper because any prophet, no matter how great or how holy, is a human being and capable of speaking falsehoods as well as truth. A prophet's holiness is no guarantee that every word from the prophet's mouth is an authentic message from God.

Warnings about false prophets can be found in both the Old and New Testaments. As the church has pointed out from the time of Saint Paul to the present, prophecy needs to be examined, tested, and judged as to its authenticity.

But just as it would be folly to assume that every prophecy is from God, it would be equal folly to assume that God, who spoke through the prophets in earlier ages, has taken a twentieth-century vow of silence. It seems more likely that while humanity is tinkering with the instruments of global nuclear holocaust, God might want to get our attention before we do something we can't correct.

Prophecy, true or false, is going on all around us. Pentecostals and charismatics are making themselves heard among virtually all Christian denominations. In widely scattered parts of the world, there are claims that the Virgin Mary is appearing and delivering messages to Christian seers. Radio evangelists claim that ancient prophecies from the Old Testament reveal hidden messages for our times. Outside the church, certain persons claim to have psychic powers that enable them to foretell future events.

Comedian Bill Cosby used to do a routine in which he pretended to be Noah listening to a voice from heaven. Cosby's Noah seems flattered at first — until the voice directs him to start building a huge ark. At that point, Noah begins acting like someone who has just received a crank telephone call. With a suspicious edge in his voice, he asks, "Who is this really?"

That is a question that God's people need to ask today. We cannot simply obey every voice that proclaims itself to be the word of God, but neither can we dismiss the idea that God is trying to tell us something.

●

CHAPTER TWO

●

Ancient Holy Men and Seers

●

In the modern world, there are two fundamentally different attitudes toward prophecy. One of these might be called the fortune-teller attitude. The other is based on Holy Scripture and the traditions of Judaism and Christianity.

The fortune-teller attitude is shared by those who think of prophecy as a supernatural ability exercised by purported seers like Nostradamus and Edgar Cayce, or even Jeane Dixon — people who have claimed a supernatural ability to predict the future. Some persons even look at biblical prophecy as a means of predicting world events in our time.

But in the Judeo-Christian tradition, prophecy means something else. In the Old Testament, the classic examples of prophecy are the words of men like Isaiah, Jeremiah, and Amos. These great prophets weren't trying to predict future events but were speaking messages from God — messages aimed at restoring and strengthening the bond between Yahweh and his people. Again, in the New Testament, prophecy isn't a form of fortune-telling but is described by early Christian writers as a gift of the Holy Spirit given to members of the church for the purposes of building up the church and empowering it to proclaim the Good News revealed by Jesus.

The fortune-teller attitude is nothing new. It existed in ancient times, too. Long before the Jews emerged as a distinct nation, the idea that secret knowledge could be revealed through supernatural means was well established among many cultures of the ancient Middle East. Typically, such divination was associated with occult practices and beliefs. Among ancient peoples, and later among the Greeks and the Romans, people commonly sought oracles — spoken messages — from diviners and seers who used various methods to put themselves into ecstatic trances. The messages spoken in the trance state were believed to derive from the gods or from the spirit world.

In Mari, an ancient city on the middle Euphrates, archaeologists in 1939 dug up some twenty thousand clay tablets that had once been part of the city's royal archives. The tablets, written in the Akkadian language, contain much information about the life and religion of the people who lived there some seventeen centuries before the birth of Jesus.

Some of the tablets reveal that in the Mari culture, oracles from the god Hadad were delivered to the king Zimri-lin by a person called a *mahhu*, a word which emphasizes the ecstatic nature of the utterances.

Records from other parts of the ancient Mediterranean world reveal similar uses of oracles and divination. Several centuries after the time of King Zimri-lin, an Egyptian named Wenamon was sent by the pharaoh to the Phoenician city of Byblos to purchase cedar. Byblos, whose people were worshipers of the god Baal, was an extremely important trading center in its day. Wenamon kept a journal of his travels, which tells of a young man employed by the court at Byblos who, in an ecstatic manner, delivered oracles from the god Baal.

The ruins of Ugarit, an ancient city on what is now the Syrian coast, were discovered in 1928 and yielded several hundred texts, including some containing evidence of ecstatic, oracular practices during the period from 4000 to 2500 B.C. And records show that in the ancient city of Hamath, near Damascus, the king told of receiving favorable oracles through seers and diviners.

Divination and oracles were a significant feature of Greek and Roman culture from the earliest times until the fourth century A.D. The Greeks and the Romans consulted the gods in almost everything they did. Oracles, spoken in human language, were an important part of this process. A person, in an ecstatic state, would

become possessed by the gods who would then speak
through the person as an intermediary.

It is not clear just when and how prophecy began
among the Jews. The Jewish historian Josephus, writing
at about the time of Christ's passion, declared that there
had been a succession of prophets in Israel from the time
of Moses (about 1250 B.C.) until the time of the Persian
king Artaxerxes I, who reigned between 464 and 424 B.C.
Our best source of information about prophecy among
the early Israelites is the Old Testament.

The Hebrew word for "prophet" is *nabi*, which,
translated literally, means mouthpiece. In the earliest
books of the Bible, *nabi* is used to mean "spokesman"
regardless of whether the *nabi* is a spokesman for
Yahweh or another human being.

God's first human spokesman in the Old Testament
is Moses. In the Book of Genesis, Moses encounters God
for the first time as a voice that speaks to him from a
burning bush. God declares that he is going to send Moses
to Egypt's pharaoh to lead his chosen people, the Jews,
out of Egypt and into a land "flowing with milk and
honey."

This message of liberation is good news, but Moses
protests. He doesn't see himself as being capable of
rescuing his kinfolk. God listens patiently to Moses'
objections and promises to perform signs to convince the
pharaoh that Moses has been sent by God. But Moses still
protests, asking Yahweh to send someone else instead.
At that point, God becomes angry but agrees to send
Moses' kinsman Aaron to be Moses' *nabi*. Moses was to
be God's mouthpiece and Aaron was to be Moses'

mouthpiece. "He shall speak to the people for you: he shall be your spokesman, and you shall be as God to him," Yahweh declares (see Exodus 4:14-16).

There were other Jews in Moses' time whom the Bible refers to as prophets. Besides Aaron, there was Aaron's sister, Miriam (described as a "prophetess" in Exodus 15:20). Scripture doesn't tell us anything about her prophecies but describes how, with a tambourine, she led other women in singing, dancing, and praising the Lord for the Jews' deliverance from Egypt.

In addition to Moses, Aaron, and Miriam, there were other ancient Israelites who prophesied. The Old Testament Book of Numbers tells how God gave Moses some relief from his labors and responsibilities by commanding him to gather seventy of the elders of Israel into the meeting tent. There, God took "some of the spirit that was on Moses" and bestowed it on the elders (see Numbers 11:16-24).

As the spirit came to rest on them the elders in the tent prophesied. The spirit of prophecy was bestowed on at least two other people, Eldad and Medad, elders who had missed the meeting. Apparently this caused some jealousy among Moses' followers because when one of his aides heard Eldad and Medad prophesying, he begged Moses to stop them. But Moses was delighted. He asked his aide, "Are you jealous for my sake? Would that all the people of the LORD were prophets! Would that the LORD might bestow his spirit on them all!" (Numbers 11:29).

The Book of Numbers, depicting Aaron and Miriam as being proud of their positions as prophets and jealous of their kinsman Moses, tells us: "And they said, 'Has the LORD indeed spoken only through Moses? Has he not spoken through us also?' And the LORD heard it. Now the man Moses was very meek, more than all men that were on the face of the earth. And suddenly the LORD said to Moses and to Aaron and Miriam, 'Come out, you three, to the tent of meeting.' And the three of them came out. And the LORD came down in a pillar of cloud, and stood at the door of the tent, and called Aaron and Miriam; and they both came forward. And he said, 'Hear my words: If there is a prophet among you, I the LORD make myself known to him in a vision, I speak with him in a dream. Not so with my servant Moses; he is entrusted with all my house. With him I speak mouth to mouth, clearly, and not in dark speech; and he beholds the form of the LORD. . .' " (Numbers 12:2-8).

Moses, then, was more than a seer. He was not only a spokesman for God but a man who was on intimate terms with Yahweh. Lesser prophets, like Aaron and Miriam, saw their prophetic ability as a mark of distinction; but Moses, in his humility, regarded prophecy as a gift freely given by God to those who were willing and ready to exercise it.

The Book of Deuteronomy, popularly attributed to Moses but not committed to writing until long after his death, contains a chapter devoted largely to teachings, warnings, and exhortations about prophets and prophecy. In Deuteronomy, Moses is quoted as giving this warning to the Israelites against soothsayers, fortune-tellers, or other diviners: "When you come into the land which the LORD, your God, is giving you, you shall not learn to

imitate the abominations of the peoples there. Let there
not be found among you anyone who immolates his son or
daughter in the fire, nor a fortune-teller, soothsayer,
charmer, diviner, or caster of spells, nor one who
consults ghosts and spirits or seeks oracles from the
dead. Anyone who does such things is an abomination to
the LORD, and because of such abominations the LORD,
your God, is driving these nations out of your way. You,
however, must be altogether sincere toward the LORD,
your God. Though these nations whom you are to
dispossess listen to their soothsayers and fortune-tellers,
the LORD, your God, will not permit you to do so"
(Deuteronomy 18:9-14).

Instead, says Moses, "A prophet like me will the
LORD, your God, raise up for you from among your own
kinsmen; to him you shall listen" (Deuteronomy 18:15).
This passage was understood by the Jews to apply not
only to all true prophets who would come after Moses,
but in a special sense, to the Messiah. Christians have
traditionally seen its fulfillment and completion in the
prophetic role of Jesus.

Moses concludes his discourse on prophecy with a
word of caution and some advice on discerning the
difference between true and false prophecy:

"And the LORD said to me, . . . 'But if a prophet
presumes to speak in my name an oracle that I have not
commanded him to speak, or speaks in the name of other
gods, he shall die.'

"If you say to yourselves, 'How can we recognize an
oracle which the LORD has spoken?', know that, even
though a prophet speaks in the name of the LORD, if his

oracle is not fulfilled or verified, it is an oracle which the LORD did not speak. The prophet has spoken it presumptuously, and you shall have no fear of him'' (Deuteronomy 18:17, 20-22).

There is nothing in Moses' attitude toward prophecy that smacks of the occult practices of other parts of the ancient Near East. Instead, there is a profound but simple familiarity between Yahweh and his servant. Moses didn't engage in any magic rituals in an attempt to pry secrets from God. Instead of trying to use God as a consultant, Moses simply listened to him and obeyed him. Moses prophesied only because God chose him to be his mouthpiece. This is the classic role of the prophet, and Moses was the first person in the Bible to be chosen by God to act in such a manner.

A few centuries after Moses' death, when the Book of Deuteronomy was written, its author declared that since the time of Moses' death "no prophet has arisen in Israel like Moses'' (Deuteronomy 34:10). There is, in fact, little mention of prophecy in the Old Testament from the time Deuteronomy was written until about the time of the beginning of the kingship of Saul, shortly before 1000 B.C. The founding of Saul's kingship is related in the First Book of Samuel, in which prophecy appears to have become an established institution in Israel.

At that time, despite the warnings attributed to Moses, the prophecy of the Jews had become somewhat similar to the oracular practices of other cultures in the ancient Near East. The Old Testament shows that there were Hebrew prophets in Israel who, like the people of neighboring lands, delivered oracles after working themselves into ecstatic states through singing and dancing.

These were bands of prophets, referred to sometimes as the "sons of the prophet." They attached themselves as disciples to a holy man or prophet who acted as their spiritual teacher. They are sometimes referred to in the Books of Samuel and Kings as "guild prophets" and they are believed to have exercised some kind of liturgical function, although this function is not clearly defined in the historical books of the Old Testament.

Prophets of another sort existed at that time, too — "court prophets" whom kings employed and consulted before making decisions. An example of this occurs in the First Book of Kings. Ahab, king of Israel, contemplating a military campaign, gathers some four hundred prophets and asks them, "Shall I go to attack Ramoth-gilead or shall I refrain?" The prophets were unanimous. "Go up," they advised. "The LORD will deliver it over to the king" (see 1 Kings 22:6).

But Ahab apparently wasn't satisfied and looked about for other prophets to consult. Reluctantly, he sent for a prophet named Micaiah, even though he hated the man. Micaiah, unlike the other prophets, foretold a military disaster for Ahab. It was an unfortunate encounter for both the king and the prophet. Because he had foretold defeat, Micaiah was sent to prison; and the king, instead of heeding Micaiah's prophecy, went off to battle and was killed.

After Moses, the first biblical figure whose prophetic ministry is described in some detail is Samuel, a famous

holy man who lived and prophesied around 1040 B.C., some
two centuries after the time of Moses.

The First Book of Samuel makes clear that from the
time he was conceived, Samuel was set apart for a
special mission to God. His mother, Hannah, unable to
conceive a child, prays to Yahweh asking for a son and
promising that if God answers her request she, in turn,
will give the child to the service of God.

Hannah's prayers are answered and when the child is
born she names him Samuel (literally, "name of God").
After he is weaned, his mother, true to her word,
entrusts him to Eli, a priest in the temple at Shiloh,
where in those days the Ark of the Covenant was kept.
After Hannah has thus given her son to God, she offers a
prayer of praise, strikingly similar to the Magnificat, the
song of praise offered by Mary when she was pregnant
with Jesus. While Samuel is still a boy, he begins to hear
God speaking to him.

One night he is awakened by a voice that he imagines
to be Eli's. Three times he hears the voice and runs to Eli
in response. Finally, Eli realizes what is happening and
tells Samuel, "Go to sleep, and if you are called, reply,
'Speak, LORD, for your servant is listening' " (1 Samuel
3:9).

Samuel follows Eli's instructions and, in return, he
receives a somber message from Yahweh. God tells
Samuel he is angry because Eli's sons have blasphemed
and Eli has failed to reprove them. Young Samuel is
directed by God to tell the priest that no sacrifice or
offering will remove the family's guilt.

Like many another prophet, Samuel finds the

message a hard one to deliver, but, at Eli's insistence, he delivers the message accurately.

The incident reveals some of the unique characteristics that separated Jewish prophecy from oracular traditions of other ancient cultures. Samuel didn't go looking for divine messages; rather, it was God who initiated the episode. In fact, it took three attempts by God and a bit of instruction from Eli before Samuel even began to get the message. Again, there was no ritual magic used in an attempt to make God speak. Another difference is that the message was not intended to give Samuel or Eli any kind of advantage in human endeavors. It was a hard message for Samuel to deliver and a hard one for Eli to hear. Its sole purpose was to remind Eli of his obligations to God.

Other prophets of Samuel's time, like the diviners of neighboring lands, exercised their gift in an ecstatic manner. Often, they would sing and dance until they reached an ecstatic or prophetic state. It was believed that prophets in such a state were seized by the power of God, who enabled them to speak truths hidden from other persons. Samuel himself later presided over a band of such prophets. But, like Moses, Samuel appears to have communicated more intimately with God than they did. The Old Testament declares, ''. . . the LORD was with him and let none of his words fall to the ground. And all Israel from Dan to Beer-sheba knew that Samuel was established as a prophet of the LORD'' (1 Samuel 3:19-21).

The same chapter that tells of God speaking to Samuel in the night declares that such events were considered unusual in Samuel's time. A verse added to the original text by some ancient Hebrew editor asserts, "Now the boy Samuel was ministering to the LORD under Eli. And the word of the LORD was rare in those days; there was no frequent vision" (1 Samuel 3:1).

The Old Testament depicts Samuel not only as a *nabi* (prophet) but also as an *is-elohim* (man of God) and a *hoszeh* (seer). He had a reputation of being able not only to prophesy but to "see" hidden things through supernatural power. For example, when Saul, the son of a Benjaminite named Kish, goes looking for some lost asses that had strayed away from his father's herd, a servant suggests that they consult Samuel because of his reputation as a seer (see 1 Samuel 9:3-10).

In another of those biblical editorial comments, the text explains, "In former times in Israel, anyone who went to consult God used to say, 'Come, let us go to the seer.' For he who is now called prophet was formerly called seer" (1 Samuel 9:9).

The idea of "consulting" God in such a manner is more closely related to the traditions of non-Jewish cultures than to the prophetic tradition that was to evolve later in Israel.

It is significant that when Saul and his servant came to Samuel, the "seer" told them not to worry about the lost asses — that they had already been found. Samuel had more important things to tell Saul. As it turned out, the Lord had already revealed to Samuel that he was raising Saul up to be a leader of Israel.

Here, then, is a perfect example of the difference between the "fortune-teller" concept and the Judeo-Christian view of prophecy. Even though Samuel had a reputation as a seer, his more important ministry was as a mouthpiece for God. Through Samuel, God made known his plan to raise up Saul as a leader of Israel. Through Samuel, God warned the people and King Saul to be faithful and obedient. It was through Samuel that God directed Saul to attack the city of Amalek and, when Saul refused, it was Samuel who prophesied that because Saul had broken God's command, his kingdom would not endure.

Samuel did all this as a servant of God, rather than as a servant of Saul, the king. The messages he spoke to Saul weren't given in order to please Saul or to satisfy Saul's curiosity. That would have amounted to little more than fortune-telling. Samuel's prophecies had another purpose: to make known the will of God.

Yahweh, the Holy One of Israel, clearly did not want his people to confuse prophecy with magic. The Mosaic law forbade the Jews, under penalty of death, to consult fortune-tellers and mediums or to practice various forms of divination. The God of the Israelites was a God who put his word into the mouths of prophets. He had no need to communicate through fortune-tellers, necromancers, the entrails of sacrificed animals, or any of the methods practiced by diviners. Yahweh was, as Moses had perceived, a God who yearned to speak directly to his people — if they would but learn to listen and heed his word. And yet, the Israelites, in times of personal or national distress, often fell back into the occult practices that were common in their part of the world.

As a faithful Jew and as king, Saul sought to drive fortune-tellers out of the land, yet even Saul was not

immune to the temptation to seek after knowledge
through forbidden means. After Samuel died, Saul
yearned for someone who could tell him the truth. When
a Philistine army gathered against Israel, the
disheartened Saul desperately sought a message from
God. The Old Testament declares that he "consulted the
LORD; but the LORD gave no answer, whether in dreams
or by the Urim[1] or through prophets" (1 Samuel 28:6).

After Saul had exhausted every legal means of trying
to pry some knowledge out of God, he sent his servants
out to see if perhaps some fortune-teller or medium had
survived the purges he had ordered. They told him that in
the city of Endor, there lived a necromancer — a woman
who purportedly could conjure up spirits of dead persons
for consultation by her clients.

The woman was afraid of being put to death if she
told Saul's fortune, but Saul eventually persuaded her to
summon up Samuel's ghost. When the ghost appeared,
Saul poured out his troubles: "I am in great straits, for
the Philistines are waging war against me and God has
abandoned me," Saul lamented. "Since he no longer
answers me through prophets or in dreams, I have called
you to tell me what I should do" (see 1 Samuel 28:15).

As might be expected, the ghost didn't give Saul any
welcome news. The ghost told Saul that God "has torn
the kingdom from your grasp and has given it to your
neighbor David." The ghost added, "By tomorrow you
and your sons will be with me, and the LORD will have
delivered the army of Israel into the hands of the
Philistines" (see 1 Samuel 28:17, 19). In the battle that
followed, Saul's army was defeated and he killed himself

to avoid being captured and tortured by the Philistines.

Among the other prophets of the early Old Testament period were Elijah, who lived some nine centuries before the birth of Christ, and Elijah's disciple, Elisha. Elijah, one of the greatest religious figures in the history of Israel, is best known for his defense of the Jewish religion against Queen Jezebel, who tried to force the Israelites to worship the god Baal.

Baal was a fertility god of the Canaanites who sought his blessing with rituals that included sexual union between worshipers and temple prostitutes. The cult of Baal had its prophets, too, but was at odds with the religion of the Jews, not only because the Jews regarded it as obscene, but because it treated religion as nothing more than a way of influencing nature. The cult of Baal was making strong inroads among the Jews when Elijah appeared about the beginning of the ninth century B.C. The conflicts between the two religions are not unlike the conflicts we see today between those who seek the word of God and those who dabble in the occult. The Bible dramatizes the struggle as a contest between Elijah and the prophets of Baal.

Elijah was a man of God credited with the ability to work miracles as well as to prophesy. The First Book of Kings tells stories of how Elijah multiplied flour and oil and raised a dead child to life. But even more than that, he was a man consumed with faithfulness to the living God.

Yet, during his lifetime, Elijah had seen a disturbing spread of Baal worship among his kinsmen. Jezebel, a Tyrian wife of Ahab and a worshiper of Baal, had begun murdering the prophets of Yahweh. It was at that point that Elijah predicted to Ahab that there was to be a severe drought in Israel.

That forecast didn't do anything for Elijah's popularity with the king. Elijah's life must have been in danger because the Lord commanded the prophet to go and hide himself in the countryside. But three years later, at the height of the drought, as 1 Kings 18 tells us, the Lord spoke to Elijah, saying, "Go, show yourself to Ahab; and I will send rain upon the earth."

When Ahab saw Elijah, he denounced him as a "troubler of Israel," but the prophet boldly declared, "I have not troubled Israel, but you have, and your father's house, because you have forsaken the commandments of the LORD and followed the Baals" (see 1 Kings 18:18).

Then Elijah arranged a contest between himself and some four hundred fifty prophets of Baal. "Let two bulls be given to us," he told the assembled Jews. "Let them choose one for themselves, and cut it in pieces and lay it on the wood, but put no fire to it; and I will prepare the other bull and lay it on the wood, and put no fire to it" (see 1 Kings 18:23).

Then he said to the prophets of Baal, "You shall call on your gods and I will call on the LORD. The God who answers with fire is God." And all the people agreed. (See 1 Kings 18:24.)

All morning long, the other prophets cried out to Baal, begging him to answer them. They hopped and danced around the altar they had prepared. When nothing happened, Elijah taunted them. "Call louder," he said. "Perhaps he is asleep and must be awakened." The Bible declares that "they cried aloud, and cut themselves after their custom with swords and lances, until the blood gushed upon them. And as midday passed, they raved on until the time of the offering of the oblation, but there was no voice; no one answered, no one heeded." (See 1 Kings 18:26-29.)

When it was Elijah's turn, he had the people pour water on the wood he had prepared. Then he prayed, "LORD, God of Abraham, Isaac, and Israel, let it be known this day that you are God in Israel and that I am your servant and have done all these things by your command. Answer me, LORD! Answer me, that this people may know that you, LORD, are God and that you have brought them back to their senses" (1 Kings 18:36-37). When he finished praying, the "LORD's fire" (lightning) came down and consumed the holocaust. The people fell on the ground and declared that Yahweh was God.

The episode sounds almost like a contest between rival magicians. On the surface, it seems as if the only difference between Yahweh and Baal is that Yahweh could be commanded with more success. Yet the opposite is true. Notice Elijah's words: "let it be known this day that you are God in Israel and that I am your servant and have done all these things by your command" (1 Kings 18:36). It was not a case of Elijah commanding God to act; rather, it was the other way around: it was God commanding Elijah to act.

The difference between prophecy and magic is similar. In genuine prophecy, it is God who speaks; no one else.

CHAPTER THREE

'Classic' Prophets and the Word of God

Some people think "prophecy" means predicting the future, but there's more to it than that. Anyone who has trouble telling the difference between prophecy and mere fortune-telling should read and become familiar with the great prophets of the Old Testament — Amos, Isaiah, Hosea, Jeremiah, and others. The words they spoke did more than predict. They shaped the destiny not only of Israel but of the entire world.

For more than two centuries, while Israel underwent some of the greatest trials of its history, these prophets proclaimed the word of God so powerfully that their words became a permanent part of Scripture.

The "great age of prophecy" began in about 750 B.C. with the prophecies of Amos and lasted for more than two hundred years. The prophets of that age are known as the "classic prophets" of the Bible. They were a far different breed from the earlier guild prophets, who had delivered oracles while in ecstatic trances. The classic prophets were also distinctly different from the court prophets, who were employed by kings and other political leaders. The first allegiance of a court prophet was to his king. The only allegiance of the classic prophets was to God.

The prophecies of the professional guild prophets and court prophets had been, in some ways, similar to the oracles of other ancient cultures, but those of the classic prophets are unique in their revelation of God's word and his concern for humanity.

By the time Amos began his prophetic ministry, Israel had already gone through several stages in the development of prophecy. As mentioned earlier, the Hebrew word for prophet is *nabi*, but the word had various shades of meaning that changed somewhat over the course of Jewish history.

To Amos, the first of the classic prophets of Israel, *nabi* was almost a dirty word. To understand why, we must look briefly at the history of ancient Israel and, in particular, at the times in which Amos lived and prophesied.

The history of the Jews as a distinct people begins

around 1850 B.C. with the arrival of their ancestor
Abraham in Canaan. The Book of Genesis tells how God
spoke to Abraham and made a covenant with him,
promising that Abraham's descendants would possess
the land of Canaan.

Genesis tells us that during a period of famine in
Canaan, the patriarch Jacob and his sons moved to
Egypt. Historians believe this would have been
sometime around 1700 B.C. The descendants of Jacob
prospered in Egypt for several centuries, according to
Genesis, and as their numbers increased, the Egyptians
began to fear and persecute them.

At that time, they were an ethnic minority without a
land of their own. Their first large step toward
nationhood was taken when Moses, their great prophetic
leader, safely led them out of Egypt and back to Canaan,
the land where their nomadic ancestors had lived.

The Exodus not only marks the birth of the Jewish
nation but underscores the relationship that was
established between that nation and God. Moses was the
hero of the Exodus, but the event depended on more than
one man's heroism. Scripture depicts the Exodus as
God's plan, not Moses', and its miraculous success didn't
depend on the brilliance of Moses' leadership but his
obedience to God.

For the Jews, the Exodus became an unmistakable
sign that God was still faithful to the covenant he had
made with their ancestor Abraham. Time and again, the
authors of the Old Testament looked back to the Exodus
and kept the Jews aware that it was by this great act of

salvation that God had rescued them and made them a
nation.

But nationhood didn't burst into full bloom as soon as
the Jews arrived as a people in Canaan. When they got
there, the Jews were not yet a united people but a loose
tribal organization. From about 1200 to 1000 B.C. these
tribal groups were led by a series of "judges" — tribal
leaders whom they regarded as divinely appointed. The
tribes of Israel, threatened by the Philistines in about
1000 B.C., became a kingdom under the leadership of Saul,
but the kingdom didn't last. With the death of King
Solomon in about 931 B.C., Israel was divided into two
kingdoms — Israel in the north and Judah in the south.
When Amos began his prophetic ministry in the eighth
century B.C., the Jews were still a divided people,
bordered on three sides by more powerful nations: Egypt
to the south and Syria to the north; on the east there were
marauding tribes and beyond those, Babylon and the
mighty empire of Assyria.

The Israelites were aware of their own weakness and
the power of their neighbors, but they weren't alarmed.
For almost a hundred years, Egypt and Assyria had been
too preoccupied with internal problems to wage war
against the Jews. Israel, the northern kingdom, had won
some wars against weaker nations, giving the people a
false sense of security. After nearly a century without
any serious threats from outside, the two kingdoms had
grown complacent about the threat of invasion.

The Jews felt even less threatened by danger from
within. Yet decadence and corruption were rampant. A
caste system had developed, separating the rich from the

poor. In their quest for material wealth and luxury, the people had grown insensitive to God's love of justice and blind to the social evils of their day.

In the northern kingdom, ruthless and greedy leaders were in power and many of the people had fallen under the influence of immigrants who worshiped pagan gods. The worship of Baal, which had persisted for more than four hundred years, was once again on the increase.

In the south, the people were complacent and few of their leaders ever reminded them of the covenant God had made with them. Even the temple worship of the Jews had degenerated into meaningless rituals in which men and women sought to appease Yahweh with animal sacrifices instead of simply acknowledging him and worshiping him as God.

The "prophets" of that age were professional advisers, hired by kings. They didn't speak on God's behalf, although they sometimes claimed to. Their chief purpose was to give counsel to the king and they usually told the king what he wanted to hear.

It was into this milieu of corruption, indolence, and apostasy that a shepherd named Amos was sent by Yahweh to admonish his people and to warn of God's anger and of the disaster that awaited Israel on the mighty and terrible "Day of the Lord."

Amos was a native of Judah, the southern kingdom. Before he became a prophet, he was a shepherd in and around Tekoa, a town ten miles south of Jerusalem on barren heights that overlook the Dead Sea and the arid wilderness that surrounds it.

In the Book of Amos, the prophet describes himself

not only as a shepherd but also as a gatherer of sycamore fruit (see Amos 7:14). The sycamores of the Old Testament were actually a form of wild fig tree whose fruit was fed to livestock or, perhaps, eaten by the poor.

There is no mention of a family in the Book of Amos and it is easy to imagine him as a man who spent many hours, perhaps days on end, tending his flocks in the wilderness. His words are filled with images from the desert, revealing a man who was in touch with nature and aware of nature's ways.

But Amos didn't remain in the desert forever. He traveled north — to places like Samaria, Gilgal, and Bethel. He probably went there originally to sell wood, but it was also in the north that he began exercising the prophetic ministry that has earned him a permanent place in the history of Judaism and Christianity.

It is easy to imagine this man of the desert being repulsed and disheartened by the corruption that he observed in the north. But he was a fearless and independent man who was unafraid to speak the truth, no matter how harsh.

During his days alone in the desert, he had developed a love of God and had learned to listen to him. Amos spoke out against corruption because God told him to and, inevitably, he got into trouble for doing so.

Amos began his prophetic ministry during the reign of King Jeroboam II. He spoke his oracles, at least some of them, at the large shrine of Bethel, some fourteen miles north of Jerusalem. The oracles and teachings of Amos, compiled either by him or by some of his disciples, are found in the Book of Amos, the oldest of the prophetic books of the Old Testament.

Bethel had been, among other things, a center of prophetic activity, but no earlier prophets delivered the kinds of prophecies that Amos spoke. His scathing oracles denounced the hollow prosperity of the northern kingdom, the widespread injustice that was so obvious to him, the exploitation of the poor, the intrusion of pagan practices, and the substitution of mere ceremony for genuine worship.

His message was more than the officials of Israel were willing to tolerate. Amaziah, the priest in charge of the shrine at Bethel, sent word to King Jeroboam that Amos had prophesied that "Jeroboam shall die by the sword, / and Israel must go into exile away from his land" (Amos 7:11).

Ever since the Exodus, the land of Israel had held a special significance for the Jews as a sign of God's faithfulness to his covenant. What business did this shepherd from the south have to predict the loss of what God had given?

The priest kicked Amos out of the shrine and told him to go back to the south. "O seer," he told the prophet, "go, flee away to the land of Judah, and eat bread there, and prophesy there; but never again prophesy at Bethel, for it is the king's sanctuary, and it is a temple of the kingdom" (see Amos 7:12-13). Amos was insulted at being referred to as a prophet, for the prophets of his time had become little more than professional seers who were more interested in their fees than in God's word. Amos scathingly replied, "I am no prophet, nor a

prophet's son; but I am a herdsman, and a dresser of
sycamore trees, and the LORD took me from following the
flock, and the LORD said to me, 'Go, prophesy to my
people Israel' " (Amos 7:14-15).

To Amaziah, Amos must have seemed to be
challenging both the king and the very faithfulness of
God. Yet it was not God's faithfulness to the covenant
that Amos was challenging but Israel's. And no prophet
in Israel had ever spoken this way before.

Amos was the first prophet to declare that Israel's
unique relationship with God did not exempt the Jewish
nation from God's judgment. It was not enough to be
chosen by God, Amos insisted. By straying from God's
ways, Israel had failed to honor Yahweh. He is also the
first of the prophets to show any concern on the part of
God for the sins of other nations. To Amos, these, too,
were children of God. Damascus, Tyre, Edom, Ammon,
and Moab had each, in its own way, committed crimes
that God would punish. But Israel's guilt, he declared,
was more serious because Israel had been shown the
light of God's love.

Speaking in the name of Yahweh, Amos declares to
Israel, "You alone have I favored, / more than all the
families of the earth; / Therefore I will punish you for all
your crimes" (Amos 3:2).

Amos knew Yahweh as a God who could not permit
himself to be overcome by evil. Therefore, all the
injustice, false piety, and indolence would bring God's
judgment against Israel. The shepherd of Tekoa could
see what was coming just as surely as if he were back in
the desert watching storm clouds gather over his flock.

The tone of the Book of Amos is threatening. He was a prophet of judgment, not redemption. Again, speaking in the name of the Lord, he declares: "The eyes of the Lord GOD are on this sinful kingdom; / I will destroy it from the face of the earth" (Amos 9:8).

The only message of hope in the Book of Amos comes at the very end. In an epilogue, God promises that after the destruction and exile, he will raise the nation up under the leadership of a messianic king, never again to be "plucked from the land I have given them." Many scholars believe that this "happy ending" was written by someone other than Amos and was added to alleviate the harsh judgment proclaimed by Amos.

Amos was the first, but by no means the last, of the classic prophets of the Old Testament. Four of the prophetic books of the Old Testament — Isaiah, Jeremiah, Ezekiel, and Daniel — are frequently referred to as "the major prophets." That title is a little misleading. It seems to refer to the stature of those men as the greatest of the prophets, but, actually, it simply refers to the fact that the books which bear their names are longer than those of the so-called "minor prophets": Amos, Hosea, Micah, Zephaniah, Nahum, Habakkuk, Haggai, Zechariah, Obadiah, Malachi, Joel, and Jonah.

In most cases, these were the actual names of real prophets, although there is some doubt as to whether they are the actual authors of all of the Scripture verses that are attributed to them.

The Book of Isaiah contains prophecies dating back almost to the time of Amos as well as prophecies from the time of the exile, about a hundred years later.

Although all of these are attributed to Isaiah, a prophet who lived in Jerusalem before the exile, different writing styles indicate the book had at least two different authors.

One of the Old Testament prophets, Daniel, may have been a fictional character rather than an actual person. Although the Book of Daniel is set in the period of the Babylonian exile, scholars generally agree that it was composed much later by an author who had limited knowledge of the exile. Moreover, although Christians have traditionally grouped the book with the major prophets, the Hebrew Bible does not. The book more closely resembles the apocalyptic literature that emerged after the age of classic prophecy.

The classic prophets, like Amos, scorned the professional or court prophets of an earlier age. Their model was Moses. No one else in the history of Israel better exemplifies the true prophetic spirit. Like Moses, the classic prophets were not seers who dabbled in the supernatural. They prophesied for one reason only: Yahweh had revealed truth to them and they were obliged to speak on his behalf.

They didn't enunciate new religious beliefs; rather, they exhorted the Jews to rekindle their allegiance to Yahweh and his covenant. To these prophets, Yahweh was not some impersonal force that created the universe but a God who involved himself in the affairs of humanity and who, by his own choice, entered into bonds of friendship with his people. The prophets saw him as a father or husband (occasionally as a mother, too) who not only cared about his children but who was capable of feeling such emotions as tenderness, compassion, and anger — depending on the way his children responded to his love.

Through the prophets, God revealed himself as a person — a person who wanted his children to be righteous. The prophets believed that the only way to live in the fullness of God's love was to obey that call to righteousness. That belief is beautifully summed up by the prophet Micah: "He has showed you, O man, what is good; / and what does the LORD require of you / but to do justice, and to love goodness, / and to walk humbly with your God?" (Micah 6:8).

The classic prophets were men with a mission, delegated by God to speak in his name. Typically, they were reluctant to accept God's call. Like Moses they were often unwilling to do what God was asking of them. Usually, they saw themselves as untalented persons whose warnings and exhortations would be rejected by the people. True prophets of Yahweh got in trouble with kings and other public officials. Theirs was a thankless task, a task they accepted only out of obedience to God.

In many of the prophetic books, the prophet's call is revealed in symbolic images. For Isaiah, the call came with a vision of angels:

"In the year that King Uzziah died I saw the Lord sitting upon a throne, high and lifted up; and his train filled the temple. Above him stood the seraphim; each had six wings: with two he covered his face, and with two he covered his feet, and with two he flew. And one called to another and said:

" 'Holy, holy, holy is the LORD of hosts;
     the whole earth is full of his glory.'
"And the foundations of thresholds shook at the voice
of him who called, and the house was filled with smoke.
And I said: 'Woe is me! For I am lost; for I am a man of
unclean lips, and I dwell in the midst of a people of
unclean lips; for my eyes have seen the King, the LORD of
hosts!' " (Isaiah 6:1-5).

[Remember that among the Jews it was popularly
believed that one could not gaze upon the face of God and
live. But the prophet, like Moses, dealt with God face-to-
face.]

"Then flew one of the seraphim to me, having in his
hand a burning coal which he had taken with tongs from
the altar. And he touched my mouth, and said: 'Behold,
this has touched your lips; your guilt is taken away, and
your sin forgiven.' And I heard the voice of the Lord
saying, 'Whom shall I send, and who will go for us?' Then
I said, 'Here am I! Send me' " (Isaiah 6:6-8).

The touching of a burning coal to Isaiah's lips
symbolizes the purification that makes the prophet
worthy of his call. The call of Isaiah has a parallel in the
call of the prophet Ezekiel; however, what touched
Ezekiel's lips was not a burning coal but a scroll,
symbolizing the word of God. Ezekiel tells of a vision in
which the voice of God commanded him to eat the scroll.

"So I opened my mouth, and he gave me the scroll to
eat. And he said to me, 'Son of man, eat this scroll that I
give you and fill your stomach with it.' Then I ate it; and
it was in my mouth as sweet as honey.

"And he said to me, 'Son of man, go, get you to the

house of Israel, and speak with my words to them. . .' "
(Ezekiel 3:2-4).

When Jeremiah received his call, Yahweh himself
put his hand on the prophet's mouth and said, "Behold, I
have put my words in your mouth" (see Jeremiah 1:9).

Emboldened by such encounters with the living God,
the prophets spoke without mincing words. Those who
prophesied before the exile (Amos, Hosea, Nahum,
Habakkuk, Micah, Isaiah, and Jeremiah) warned Israel
of her sins and of the justice that God delivers against
those who do evil.

Hosea, although he condemned Israel's sins, was as
compassionate and hopeful as Amos was austere. He was
a man whose wife had abandoned him for other lovers,
but he loved her still and, in his yearning for her, he saw
a reflection of God's desire for reunion with his people.

Isaiah (in this case we refer to the man of Jerusalem
whose prophecies are contained in the first sections of
the Book of Isaiah) was a man whose words were first
addressed to a nation threatened by the mighty armies of
Assyria. He counseled faith in God, reminding the people
that God and his justice would outlast Israel's enemies.
Isaiah inspired his listeners with his visions of an age
when God's peace and justice would flourish under a
messianic king.

Micah, who was a contemporary of Isaiah's, foresaw
the destruction of Israel and pleaded with God to show
mercy.

Jeremiah, whose prophecies were collected and
written down by his secretary, Baruch, barely escaped

the death penalty for his strongly worded predictions of disaster.

Ezekiel marks a turning point in the history of prophecy. He was among the Israelites who were taken to Babylon as captives and was the first to receive his prophetic call in a foreign land.

Prophesying to the Jews in Babylon, he warned that the worst was yet to come — that Jerusalem itself, considered by the Jews to be inviolable, would be destroyed. His countrymen didn't believe him, but his words were proven true when Nebuchadnezzar laid waste to the holy city in 587 B.C. and destroyed the temple, the geographical center of Jewish worship.

After the destruction of Jerusalem, Ezekiel continued to prophesy, but his words had a new theme: the promise of a new covenant under which God would restore his people.

The Jews remained in exile until 539 when the armies of the Persian king Cyrus II liberated them and returned to them the sacred vessels of the temple that Nebuchadnezzar had looted. Soon after their return from exile, the Jews built a new temple, as large as its predecessor but not as rich in decoration.

The prophetic books that were written after the exile include the sayings of Zephaniah, Haggai, Zechariah, Obadiah, Joel, and Malachi. They are largely devoted to solving the problems that faced the Jewish nation on its return and do not possess the powerful imagery that characterized the preexilic prophets. The Book of Haggai urged the rebuilding of the temple at Jerusalem while those of Zechariah and Joel kept alive the hope of a new messianic kingdom.

During the five centuries that followed the return from exile, the prophetic ministry gradually declined. The postexilic prophets didn't speak with the urgency and vigor that characterized the prophets before the exile.

In the Jewish world after the exile, the word of God was increasingly interpreted through the writings of priests and scribes, rather than revealed through the spoken word of the prophets.

But the day was coming when the word of God would be fully revealed — not merely in speech but in the very being of someone who was more than a prophet.

●

CHAPTER FOUR

●

The Person Who IS the Word of God

●

For centuries, the Jews had anticipated the coming of the Messiah, the anointed one, who would establish an Israelite empire — a world that would live in peace, justice, and harmony with Yahweh.

Such expectations had their earliest roots in the story of God's promises to Abraham of the blessings of nationhood and the growth of Israel. The reigns of David and of Solomon had fulfilled many of those expectations, but as Israel's fortunes declined, the people looked for a new David, a Messiah who would restore the nation.

The prophets had developed this theme into an expectation that Yahweh would one day raise up a new king, a political leader descended from David, who, although human, would be an agent of Yahweh and would preside over an age of peace, harmony, and obedience to God.

But after the exile, prophecy began to disappear in Israel. The Book of Malachi, the last prophetic book of the Old Testament to be written, was probably composed after the rebuilding of the temple in 516 B.C. After Malachi there were no more prophets or, at least, none whose stature and sayings are included in Holy Scripture.

In the third century B.C., Israel had fallen under Greek domination and terrible persecution that included pagan desecration of the temple at Jerusalem.

In the First Book of Maccabees, written about 100 B.C., there is a touching verse, often cited as evidence that during the persecution, prophecy had ceased to exist among the Jews. The book tells how the Jews, under Judas Maccabeus, set out to restore the temple and the altar that had been defiled by the Seleucid Kings: "And they thought it best to tear it down, lest it bring reproach upon them, for the Gentiles had defiled it. So they tore down the altar, and stored the stones in a covenient place on the temple hill until there should come a prophet to tell what to do with them" (1 Maccabees 4:45-46).

An even more revealing passage occurs in the ninth chapter: "Thus there was great distress in Israel, such as had not been since the time that prophets ceased to appear among them" (1 Maccabees 9:27).

And again, in Chapter 14: "And the Jews and their priests decided that Simon should be their leader and high priest for ever, until a trustworthy prophet should arise" (1 Maccabees 14:41).

The Jewish historian Josephus, born at about the time of Christ's death and resurrection, is the source of much of our knowledge of life in Israel from the end of the exile until A.D. 70. Writing in the first century, he tells of an unbroken succession of prophets from Moses to the time of Artaxerxes I. By Josephus's reckoning, that would have placed the end of the prophetic era at around 425 B.C. Rabbinic texts from the first century A.D. also show a common belief that prophecy had ceased or at least become dormant during the last few centuries before the birth of Christ.

Some modern scholars contend that prophecy didn't actually cease during the second-temple period (516 B.C. — A.D. 70) but took a different form and continued to influence the religious life of Judaism.

The Essenes at Qumran, for instance, whose religious beliefs and practices have been revealed through the discovery of the Dead Sea Scrolls, believed strongly that the Spirit of Yahweh was present among them. In Israel, the presence of the Spirit of Yahweh was almost synonymous with the presence of prophecy. The writings produced by the Qumran community for about a century prior to A.D. 66 suggest that they probably regarded prophecy as a normal part of their life as a religious community.

Many scholars believe there was a link between the

community at Qumran and the first prophetic figure of
the New Testament — John the Baptist.

There was a Jewish tradition which held that the
coming of the Messiah would be preceded by the return
of the prophet Elijah as the last of the prophets. The New
Testament makes it clear that both John the Baptist and
Jesus were sometimes identified by the people as Elijah,
returning as a herald of the coming messianic age.

By the time John was born, Israel had become a part
of the Roman Empire. King Herod, a Jew, was on the
throne and was in the process of building a newer and
grander temple. But the real political power in Palestine
belonged to the Roman Empire. The Romans tolerated
the religion of the Jews as long as it did not pose a threat
to Caesar.

The story of John's birth, foretold by an angel,
closely parallels the stories of the birth of several other
ancient heroes of the Jewish people. His mother,
Elizabeth, was elderly and childless, just as Sarah, the
wife of Abraham, had been when she conceived Isaac and
as Hannah had been when she conceived Samuel.

When John was born, his father, Zechariah, filled
with the Holy Spirit, praised God and foretold John's role
as a prophet: "And you, child, will be called the prophet
of the Most High; / for you will go before the Lord to
prepare his ways, / to give knowledge of salvation to his
people / in the forgiveness of their sins, / through the
tender mercy of our God; / when the day shall dawn upon
us from on high / to give light to those who sit in darkness
and in the shadow of death, / to guide our feet into the
way of peace" (Luke 1:76-79).

As an adult, John baptized and prophesied. His baptism was a baptism of repentance and forgiveness — accompanied by the ritual of immersion in water that symbolized the cleansing power of God's forgiveness. But John wasn't the first Jew to practice baptism. The Qumran scrolls indicate that the Essenes were practicing baptism even before John did. It is possible that John learned baptism from the Essenes, and scholars generally acknowledge the possibility of a connection between John the Baptist and the Essenes.

Scripture and the topography of the Jordan Valley indicate that John baptized his followers near the place where the Jordan River flows into the Dead Sea. Scripture scholar John L. McKenzie declares that if that is so, John "could scarcely have failed to have some contact with the Qumran group; the buildings were literally within sight."

Some scholars have even assumed that John was, or had been, a member of the Qumran community. At any rate, he shared their practice of baptism and they shared his openness to the prophetic spirit of God.

John's relationship to the Essenes has not been clearly defined, but his role as a prophet has. John was a prophet, although not everyone recognized him as one. The writings of Josephus mention John the Baptist not as a prophet but as a preacher. As far as Josephus was concerned, the title of prophet was reserved for heroes of the past. Jesus, on the other hand, specifically declared John to be a prophet. Speaking to the crowds who had gone out to the desert to see John, Jesus says, "Why then did you go out — to see a prophet? A prophet indeed, and something more! It is about this man that Scripture says, / 'I send my messenger ahead of you / to prepare your way before you.' / I solemnly assure you, history has not known a man born of woman greater than John the Baptizer. Yet the least born into the kingdom of God is greater than he" (Matthew 11:9-11).

In two passages in Matthew, Jesus identifies John with the prophet Elijah:

"For all the prophets and the law prophesied until John; and if you are willing to accept it, he is Elijah who is to come. He who has ears to hear, let him hear" (Matthew 11:13-15).

"And the disciples asked him, 'Then why do the scribes say that first Elijah must come?' He replied, 'Elijah does come, and he is to restore all things; but I tell you that Elijah has already come, and they did not know him, but did to him whatever they pleased. So also the Son of man will suffer at their hands.' Then the disciples understood that he was speaking to them of John the Baptist" (Matthew 17:10-13).

For those who contended that prophecy had ceased, John's public ministry must have been difficult to explain away. The people took his words seriously, and his bizarre apparel of animal skins and his diet of insects identified him as a man who was not bound by convention. John's whole way of life was cast in the image of a prophet — a man dressed like Elijah; a man of the desert, like Amos, a man who called the people to renew their faithfulness to God.

He preached repentance, generosity to the poor, and an end to oppression and cheating. But the most

distinctive feature of his preaching was his
announcement that the Messiah was about to appear in
Israel.

"Reform your lives!" he commanded. "The reign of
God is at hand" (see Matthew 3:2).

Great crowds were coming to him to be baptized.
Mark's Gospel declares that the people of Jerusalem
went out to John in great numbers and were baptized by
him in the Jordan as they confessed their sins (see Mark
1:5). John was held in such high esteem that even the
Pharisees were afraid to publicly question his mission
(Matthew 21:25-27; Mark 11:30-33; Luke 20:4-8). In fact,
some of the Pharisees and Sadducees were among those
who went out to be baptized; whether for the sake of
appearance or from true repentance we can only
speculate.

To Herod Antipas, tetrarch of Galilee, John the
Baptist was an enemy. A Jew by birth, Herod was
educated in Rome and served in Galilee as a puppet king
and agent for the Roman emperor Tiberius. He was
expected to report to the emperor any misconduct or
disloyalty on the part of Roman officials or the other
puppet kings who, like himself, governed in the eastern
reaches of the empire.

Matthew tells us in Chapter 14 of his Gospel that
Herod married Herodias, the ex-wife of his brother
Philip. The Jews were scandalized and John the Baptist
publicly rebuked Herod for his adulterous and incestuous
behavior. John's outspoken criticism of Herod was to
cost him his life.

Herod had John thrown into prison but balked at

actually executing him. Matthew's Gospel tells us that "Herod wanted to kill John but was afraid of the people, who regarded him as a prophet" (Matthew 14:5). Herodias, however, was bolder and more cunning. While John was in prison, she gave a birthday party for Herod and during the party Herodias's daughter, Salome, danced for Herod. In an excess of admiration for her dancing ability, and probably under the influence of much wine, Herod promised to grant any request she made. Prompted by her mother, Salome said she wanted the head of John the Baptist on a platter, and Herod sent the executioners to kill John while the party went on.

While John had been alive, he was such a charismatic figure that some of the people had speculated that he was the Messiah himself. But John denied it. While he was still alive, he had declared, "I baptize you with water for repentance, but he who is coming after me is mightier than I, whose sandals I am not worthy to carry; he will baptize you with the Holy Spirit and with fire. His winnowing fork is in his hand, and he will clear his threshing floor and gather his wheat into the granary, but the chaff he will burn with unquenchable fire" (Matthew 3:11-12).

These prophetic words referred, of course, to Jesus. And in fulfillment of John's words, Jesus had one day appeared on the banks of the Jordan, along with the many others, and asked that John baptize him, too. Matthew tells us that John, at first, refused. If he considered himself unworthy to carry Christ's sandals, how could he be worthy to baptize Jesus? "I should be baptized by you," John protests, "yet you come to me!" (See Matthew 3:14.)

At his baptism, Jesus saw the Holy Spirit descend from heaven in the form of a dove and heard a voice say: "This is my beloved Son, with whom I am well pleased" (Matthew 3:17). This vision of the Holy Spirit identifies Jesus as the Son of God. At the same time, his insistence on baptism reveals Jesus as a human being who, although he had no need to repent, deliberately chose to identify himself with those who did.

The love of Jesus for sinners and social outcasts was one of the distinguishing features of his ministry. Even as he hung on the cross he demonstrated his love for the criminals who were dying on their own nearby crosses. This friendliness and familiarity of Jesus toward outcasts and sinners made it all the more difficult for many of his contemporaries to recognize him as the Messiah. The Messiah was to have been a king. Jesus just didn't fit the popular image of how a king should look or act.

But as he traveled about the countryside, healing and preaching, Jesus, like John the Baptist, began to acquire a reputation as a prophet. This reputation was strengthened among the people who witnessed the miracles he performed.

When Jesus multiplied loaves of bread and fishes in order to feed a hungry crowd, the people murmured, "This is indeed the prophet who is to come into the world!" (John 6:14). After Jesus had healed a blind man, there was a great controversy because he had done it on the Sabbath. Some of the Pharisees considered Jesus a lawbreaker, but the blind man himself had other ideas. "He is a prophet," the man told the Pharisees (see John 9:17).

On another occasion, when Jesus had raised a widow's son from the dead, the people declared, "A great prophet has arisen among us! God has visited his people" (see Luke 7:16). Luke adds, "And this report concerning him spread through the whole of Judea and all the surrounding country" (Luke 7:17).

But not everyone accepted Jesus in that role. Some could not see beyond his association with sinners, which scandalized them. There was, for instance, a Pharisee named Simon who invited Jesus to his home for dinner. It was probably a rather courageous thing for Simon to do, in view of the hostility of the Pharisee party toward Jesus.

While Simon and Jesus were eating, "a woman of the city, who was a sinner," came into the room. Quite likely, she was a prostitute. She began to anoint Jesus' feet with fragrant myrrh and as she did so, her eyes filled with tears, which fell upon Jesus' feet. Simon must have been embarrassed. Then the woman began to kiss Jesus' feet and to wipe them with her hair. Simon was shocked that Jesus did nothing to stop her. He said to himself, "If this man were a prophet he would have known who and what sort of woman this is who is touching him, for she is a sinner."

But Jesus *was* a prophet and he understood what Simon was thinking. He told Simon, "I entered your house, you gave me no water for my feet, but she has wet my feet with her tears and wiped them with her hair. You gave me no kiss, but from the time I came in she has not ceased to kiss my feet. You did not anoint my head with oil, but she has anointed my feet with ointment. Therefore I tell you, her sins, which are many, are forgiven, for she loved much; but he who is forgiven little, loves little." Then Jesus told the woman, "Your sins are forgiven." (See Luke 7:36-48.)

This touching little story reveals Jesus not only as a prophet but as something more — a person who exercised the power to forgive sins — a power that, until then, had belonged only to Yahweh. No prophet had ever before claimed such power.

Jesus never called himself a prophet, but he never denied the title either. If a prophet is a mouthpiece for God, Jesus was certainly that, but he was something more. His disciples easily recognized his prophetic nature, but they had trouble understanding the "something more."

Eventually, after John the Baptist had been executed by Herod, Jesus made them confront the question directly. "Who do people say that I am?" he asked them. The disciples couldn't agree on an answer. They told him that some of the people thought that he was John the Baptist come back to life; others thought that he was the prophet Elijah, returning to announce the dawning of the messianic age. "And you," he went on to ask, "who do you say that I am?" Only Peter grasped what he was trying to tell them. "You are the Messiah," he said. (See Mark 8:27-30.)

Yet not even Peter could grasp that Jesus was the Son of God. One day, Jesus took him, James, and John up a high mountain where Jesus' appearance dramatically changed. As the three apostles watched, his clothes became dazzling white, and Elijah and Moses — the two greatest prophets of the Old Testament — appeared and spoke to Jesus.

Overcome by awe, Peter suggested that three booths be built on the site: one for Jesus, one for Moses, and one for Elijah. The implication is that Peter recognized Jesus as one of the three greatest prophetic figures of Israel. Then a cloud overshadowed them and a voice spoke out of the cloud, echoing the words that had been spoken at the time of Jesus' baptism: "This is my Son, my beloved. Listen to him." And then they could see no one but Jesus — a prophet, yes; but something more. (See Matthew 17:1-5.)

A prophet *speaks* the word of God. Jesus certainly did that, but he did more than speak it. John's Gospel reveals that Jesus *is* the incarnate Word of God — the ultimate revelation of who God is. In that sense, Jesus is not merely a prophet but a living prophecy, spoken by God.

Other prophets spoke on God's authority, but Jesus and God are one, so he spoke on his own. When Jesus prophesied, he departed from the traditional style of prophets who usually prefaced their prophecies with phrases like, "Thus says Yahweh," so that whoever was listening knew that the message that followed was not from the prophet but from God. Jesus, however, never prefaced his messages with the words "Thus says Yahweh."

Jesus often used another phrase when he spoke:

"Amen, I say to you." It is an expression that Jesus uses more than eighty times in the Gospels, but he didn't invent it. In his time, "Amen, I say to you" was a fairly common expression used by fathers speaking to their sons, by rabbis speaking to their followers, or employers speaking to their workers. It was not the trademark of a prophet, but it was the trademark of a speaker who had the authority to teach others.

Although he didn't claim the title of prophet, Jesus, like prophets of old, reminded his hearers of the reality of God's involvement in the affairs of humanity and called them to repent. "This time is fulfilled," he prophesied at the beginning of his public ministry, "and the kingdom of God is at hand; repent, and believe in the gospel" (Mark 1:15).

As the time of his death and resurrection drew near, Jesus declared, "Truly, I say to you, there are some standing here who will not taste death before they see the kingdom of God come with power" (Mark 9:1).

Some of the things that Jesus said about prophets suggest that he strongly identified with them. When the people of his hometown of Nazareth refused to see him as anything more than a local carpenter, he quoted a popular expression of his time: "A prophet is not without honor, except in his own country, and among his own kin, and in his own house" (Mark 6:4). If that were the only time that Jesus referred to himself as a prophet, it wouldn't be very convincing. On that occasion He may have been quoting a popular saying, one which people still quote today, to emphasize the curious fact that the hometown folks are usually less impressed by their neighbors than by experts from out of town.

But there were other times when Jesus more clearly identified himself with the prophets. He was aware that in the past, many prophets had been persecuted or killed for speaking God's word to people who did not want to hear it. His own kinsman John, who had baptized him in the Jordan, was among the prophets whom the authorities had put to death, and Jesus closely identified his own rejection by the scribes and Pharisees — the Jewish religious authorities of that time — with the persecution of the prophets.

A clear example occurred after John's death while Jesus was in Herod's territory and making his way toward Jerusalem. Some Pharisees came to him and said, "Go on your way! Leave this place! Herod is trying to kill you."

Jesus replied by comparing himself to a persecuted prophet: "Go tell that fox, 'Today and tomorrow I cast out devils and perform cures, and on the third day my purpose is accomplished. For all that, I must proceed on course today, tomorrow, and the day after, since no prophet can be allowed to die anywhere except in Jerusalem' " (Luke 13:32-33).

Jerusalem, of course, was the place where the temple stood — the holy city, the symbolic dwelling place of God. And as Jesus made his way there in preparation for the climactic events of his life, his words reflect an awareness of, and an identity with, the prophets who had been killed and persecuted there:

"O Jerusalem, Jerusalem, you slay the prophets and

stone those who are sent to you! How often have I wanted to gather your children together as a mother bird collects her young under her wings, and you refused me! Your temple will be abandoned. I say to you, you shall not see me until the time comes when you say, 'Blessed is he who comes in the name of the Lord' " (Luke 13:34-35).

In that short speech, Jesus not only compares himself with the prophets but uses language that is similar in form to the oracles of the Old Testament prophets. The speech contains the elements of classic prophecy: an indictment ("you slay the prophets and stone those who are sent"), a lament ("how often I wanted to gather your children"), a judgment ("your temple will be abandoned") and a promise of salvation ("when you say, 'Blessed is he who comes in the name of the Lord' ").

When Jesus did finally enter Jerusalem, the crowds were excited. They shouted and hailed him as king. "Blessed is he who comes as king in the name of the Lord!" (See Luke 19:38.) But one didn't have to recognize Jesus as Messiah to be caught up in the excitement. News of his arrival swept through the city: "This is the prophet Jesus from Nazareth in Galilee" (Matthew 21:11).

The idea that God had raised up a prophet in their midst had taken such strong hold of the people that the Pharisees were afraid to interfere. To the people, the presence of a genuine prophet was not only a sign of God's favor but a sign of the imminence of God's kingdom.

Imminent indeed. In the final days before his

passion, Jesus foretold the destruction of Jerusalem and the temple — the end of the age. It would be a terrible time. Jesus described it in classic apocalyptic terms: stars falling from the sky, the darkening of the sun and finally, ". . . they will see the Son of man coming in clouds with great power and glory" (Mark 13:26).

Sometimes when he spoke of the temple, he made it a symbol of his own body, saying that after its destruction, it would be raised up again in three days.

It was Jesus' way of preparing his followers for the mystery of his crucifixion and resurrection, the suffering and the glory that he was to undergo and which they, as his followers, were destined to share.

On the eve of his death, he told them that "he who believes in me will also do the works that I do; and greater works than these will he do, because," as Jesus goes on to explain immediately after making this amazing claim, "I go to the Father. Whatever you ask in my name, I will do it, that the Father may be glorified in the Son. . . . I will pray the Father, and he will give you another Counselor, to be with you for ever, even the Spirit of truth, whom the world cannot receive, because it neither sees him nor knows him; you know him, for he dwells with you, and will be in you." (See John 14:12-13, 16-17.)

Later, in the same discourse, Jesus refers to this Paraclete (a Greek word for "intercessor") or Counselor as the Holy Spirit (verse 26). Toward the end of the discourse, he promises that "when the Spirit of truth comes, he will guide you into all the truth; for he will not speak on his own authority, but whatever he hears he will speak, and he will declare to you the things that are to come'' (John 16:13).

Jesus was telling his followers that even after he was gone, they would continue to do the things he had done: to heal, to preach, to proclaim the coming of the kingdom, and to prophesy. Even though they would no longer be able to see him in the flesh, he would be with them and the same Spirit that had spoken in him would be theirs.

●

●

CHAPTER FIVE

Prophecy in the Apostolic Church

●

Immediately after Jesus' death and resurrection, his disciples were struggling to make sense of what had happened. The Gospel of Luke (24:13-53) tells how, on the day of his resurrection, two of the disciples were walking to a place called Emmaus, and discussing all that had happened. Luke calls their conversation "a lively exchange."

Their master had been crucified. They did not yet understand the significance of his disappearance from his tomb.

As they talked, the risen Christ himself

approached and began to walk with them. He asked them
what they had been talking about. The two disciples did
not recognize Jesus or have any idea who this stranger
was. One of the disciples, named Cleopas, told the
stranger about the crucifixion of Jesus, "a prophet
powerful in word and deed in the eyes of God and all the
people." Cleopas went on to relate how Christ's tomb had
been found empty that very morning. It is interesting
that in spite of everything Jesus had taught and revealed
about himself, Cleopas continued to describe him merely
as "a prophet."

So Jesus, without making his identity known, taught
these two disciples again, explaining his death and
resurrection as the fulfillment of prophecy. Beginning
with Moses and all the prophets, he recounted the many
Scripture passages which had foretold the coming of the
Messiah. "How slow you are to believe all that the
prophets have announced!" he told them. "Did not the
Messiah have to undergo all this so as to enter into his
glory?"

They listened, spellbound, but still did not recognize
him. It was only later, as he ate with them, broke bread,
and gave it to them to eat that they realized who he was
— not a prophet but the Messiah — their own beloved
Lord and rabbi, risen from the dead. Later, they recalled
how their hearts had burned within them when he spoke
to them on the road. The Messiah, they now realized, was
no ordinary king who ruled by law, but one who ruled
their hearts through the breaking of bread and the
proclamation of God's word.

Appearing to them again, Jesus reminded them that

they were witnesses to his resurrection. He told them to remain in Jerusalem "until you are clothed with power from on high." And with those few words, he departed from them and was "taken up to heaven."

At that point, Luke ends his Gospel, but he continues the story of Jesus and his church in the Acts of the Apostles — Luke's account of how our church began. There are other early Christian writings that describe life in the early church but none that does so as vividly as Acts. Luke begins Chapter 1 of Acts with a retelling of how Jesus had appeared to the apostles after his resurrection: "And while staying with them he charged them not to depart from Jerusalem, but to wait for the promise of the Father, which, he said, 'you heard from me, for John baptized with water, but before many days you shall be baptized with the Holy Spirit' " (Acts 1:4-5).

Jesus' words were soon fulfilled — on the day of Pentecost (or Shabuoth, an Israelite festival that celebrates the feast of the firstfruits of the grain harvest). On the day of Pentecost, the apostles were all gathered in one place when a startling transformation took place that turned simple Galilean fishermen into prophets.

Luke describes what happened: "And suddenly a sound came from heaven like the rush of a mighty wind, and it filled all the house where they were sitting. And there appeared to them tongues as of fire, distributed and resting on each one of them. And they were all filled with the Holy Spirit and began to speak in other tongues, as the Spirit gave them utterance" (Acts 2:2-4).

This promised "baptism with the Holy Spirit"

apparently attracted a good deal of attention from the other Jews who were in Jerusalem at the time — people from various ethnic backgrounds, all of whom heard the words of the apostles in their own languages. The crowds were amazed and some even speculated that the apostles were drunk.

But Peter stood up and offered the people another explanation: ". . . these men are not drunk, as you suppose, since it is only the third hour of the day; but this is what was spoken by the prophet Joel: / 'And in the last days it shall be, God declares, / that I will pour out my Spirit upon all flesh, / and your sons and your daughters shall prophesy, / and your young men shall see visions, / and your old men shall dream dreams. . .' " (Acts 2:15-17).

And suddenly, this simple Galilean fisherman was preaching eloquently to the Jews of Jerusalem, proclaiming that Jesus was their resurrected Messiah. "This Jesus God raised up, and of that we are all witnesses," Peter declared. "Being therefore exalted at the right hand of God, and having received from the Father the promise of the Holy Spirit, he has poured out this which you see and hear" (see Acts 2:33).

Luke doesn't describe Peter's words as prophecy, but they were clearly inspired by the Holy Spirit. Peter urged his listeners to "repent, and be baptized every one of you in the name of Jesus Christ for the forgiveness of your sins; and you shall receive the gift of the Holy Spirit" (Acts 2:38).

In the days that followed, the members of the Christian community in Jerusalem began doing many of

the things Jesus had done. They healed. They preached
the Good News. And they prophesied. And as they did
these things, their community grew rapidly. These
charismatic gifts of the Holy Spirit caught the attention
of unbelievers and impressed upon them the reality of
Jesus' resurrection and presence among his followers.
According to the New Testament, the exercise of
prophecy and other charismatic gifts was not only
present but fairly common among these early Christians.
The picture that emerges from the New Testament is a
first-century church in which the charismatic gifts of
prophecy, tongues, healing, and various other Spirit-
inspired abilities were ordinary expressions of Christian
life. The gifts were a means through which God guided,
inspired, taught, and strengthened his church.

After several centuries in which Jewish prophecy
had declined, it was back in full force among the
followers of Jesus, freely distributed among the men and
women who followed him.

Luke's Acts of the Apostles is a testimony to the
work of the Holy Spirit in the apostolic church. It is filled
with evidence that the gifts of the Spirit were active and
widespread.

One of the early Christians that Luke mentions in
Acts is a man named Philip, one of seven persons chosen
on the basis of their spirituality and prudence to oversee
the community's daily distribution of food. When Luke
first mentions Philip in Acts 6:5, he describes him as "a
man full of faith and of the Holy Spirit." Later, Luke
mentions in passing that Philip "had four unmarried
daughters, who prophesied" (Acts 21:9).

We are never told that Philip was a prophet, but his house appears to have been a hotbed of prophecy. It was while Luke and Paul were visiting Philip's house that another Christian named Agabus arrived and exhibited his own gift of prophecy. Luke writes, "And coming to us he took Paul's girdle and bound his own feet and hands, and said, 'Thus says the Holy Spirit, "So shall the Jews at Jerusalem bind the man who owns this girdle and deliver him into the hands of the Gentiles" ' " (Acts 21:11).

Agabus was not a famous leader of the early Christian community. He was not an apostle. He appears to be simply an early Christian who, like Philip's daughters, had received the gift of prophecy. Acts mentions another occasion in which Agabus, in prophecy, foretold a widespread famine, enabling the Christians at Antioch to set aside whatever was needed for the relief of those who lived in Judea (see Acts 11:27-29).

The New Testament clearly makes a connection between the reception of the Holy Spirit and the manifestation of charismatic gifts. Typically, the reception of the Holy Spirit and his gifts was sought through prayer and the laying on of hands. Luke writes that in the Greek city of Ephesus Saint Paul encountered some disciples of Jesus who had received "the baptism of John" but who declared that they had not so much as heard that there was a Holy Spirit. Paul proceeded to instruct them and to baptize them in the name of Jesus.

Luke writes, "And when Paul laid his hands upon them, the Holy Spirit came on them; and they spoke with tongues and prophesied" (Acts 19:6).

Some who witnessed this apparently thought the

apostles were practicing some kind of magic. Luke tells us, for instance, of a man named Simon who had been "practicing magic" in Samaria. When Peter and John visited the area, "Simon saw that the Spirit was given through the laying on of the apostles' hands, [and] he offered them money, saying, 'Give me also this power, that any one on whom I lay my hands may receive the Holy Spirit.' " Peter scolded the man for assuming that God's gift could be bought. (See Acts 8:9-23.)

Luke also recognized that there were other spirits who sometimes spoke through the mouths of humans. In Acts 16, he tells of a slave girl in the city of Philippi who was possessed by "a spirit of divination" and was employed by her masters as a fortune-teller. When Paul and Silas visited Philippi, preaching and baptizing, they encountered this girl. Luke writes: "She followed Paul and us, crying, 'These men are servants of the Most High God, who proclaim to you the way of salvation.' And this she did for many days. But Paul was annoyed, and turned and said to the spirit, 'I charge you in the name of Jesus Christ to come out of her!' And it came out that very hour" (Acts 16:17-18).

But among the Christian prophets, it was the Holy Spirit who spoke. These prophets served in the various local churches in the apostolic age, according to Luke, presumably exercising their gifts there alongside those who taught. Luke tells us that there were several such prophets and teachers in the church at Antioch. Describing a gathering of these prophets and teachers, he writes, "While they were worshiping the Lord and fasting, the Holy Spirit said, 'Set apart for me Barnabas and Saul for the work to which I have called them.' Then after fasting and praying they laid their hands on them and sent them off" (Acts 13:2-3).

On another occasion, Luke tells how the disciples in the city of Tyre "under the prompting of the Spirit" tried to tell Paul that he should not go up to Jerusalem. It is not clear how the message was delivered, but the implication is that there were church members at Tyre who exercised some form of prophetic utterance.

While the New Testament makes it clear that the Holy Spirit spoke through early Christian prophets, it rarely quotes more than a few words of the prophecies themselves and it seldom gives details about the method by which the words were communicated.

For example, on the occasion when Barnabas and Paul were commissioned for their missionary work, we are told only *that* the Lord spoke, but not *how*.

Luke makes it clear that prophecy was not the only means used by the Lord to speak to his new church. Another way was through the use of dreams and visions. Paul, in particular, is said to have received messages from God in those ways. Acts contains three separate accounts of oracles spoken to Paul in dreams or visions.

When Paul was beginning to preach the Gospel to the Gentiles, the Lord spoke to him one night in a vision: "Do not be afraid, but speak and do not be silent, for I am with you" (see Acts 18:8-10). When Paul was in trouble with the Jewish authorities and had to be rescued by Roman soldiers, the Lord appeared at his side and said, "Take courage, for as you have testified about me at

Jerusalem, so must you bear witness also at Rome" (see Acts 23:10-11).

It is not explicitly stated in the New Testament that Paul was a prophet, but the letters he wrote to various early Christian communities and individuals show that he possessed a well-developed understanding of prophecy and its place in the church. Paul was the great teacher of the apostolic church, and his writings shed a lot of light on the use of prophecy and other charismatic gifts.

Before his conversion Paul had been a zealous persecutor of Christians, but after his conversion he considered himself one of the apostles. Unlike the twelve apostles who were personally chosen by Jesus during his earthly ministry, Paul was called to the apostolate by the risen Christ.

In his conversion Paul experienced the presence of the resurrected Christ so powerfully that he considered himself an equal of the earlier apostles. As a teacher, he surpassed them.

Many of Paul's teachings are contained in his letters to various early Christian communities and individuals. These letters constantly strive to promote the Good News of salvation in Christ and to encourage Christians to grow in faith, hope, and love. The early church recognized these writings as the inspired word of God and incorporated them into the New Testament. In fact, most of the New Testament is devoted to the letters of Saint Paul.

Paul's writings consistently reveal his gift of teaching, but his own words — as well as Luke's —

suggest that he had many of the other charismatic gifts, including those of healing and prophecy.

Paul's ability to heal is explicitly recorded in the Acts of the Apostles, but his exercise of the gift of prophecy is not as clearly described.

Paul always referred to himself as an apostle rather than a prophet. Luke includes Paul as one of a group of "prophets and teachers" in the church at Antioch (Acts 13:1), and Paul himself writes of instances in which he experienced revelations of God's word. Like the prophets of the Old Testament, Paul was a man who knew God, received his word, and delivered that word to the people. Although he didn't call himself a prophet, he was aware that some of his teachings were inspired by God while some were spoken on his own.

For example, when he wrote against divorce, he cited the teachings of Jesus, but he added teachings of his own, saying, "To the rest I say, not the Lord, that if any brother has a wife who is an unbeliever, and she consents to live with him, he should not divorce her" (see 1 Corinthians 7:10-12). Again, when he taught that widows were free to remarry, he expressed the opinion that they would be happier if they did not and added, "I think that I have the Spirit of God" (see 1 Corinthians 7:40).

Whether he considered himself an apostle or a prophet, Paul not only possessed prophetic gifts but exercised them and taught about their use. In his First Letter to the Corinthians, Paul devotes considerable attention to the proper use of the charismatic gifts and their value to the church.

Judging from this important letter of Paul's, the gifts of the Holy Spirit were such an important feature of worship among the Corinthian Christians that Paul felt obliged to step in and instruct the community in how to exercise them.

Paul stressed that different gifts are given by the Holy Spirit to the individual members of the church — which Paul described as "the body of Christ."

Paul writes: "Now there are varieties of gifts, but the same Spirit; and there are varieties of service, but the same Lord; and there are varieties of working, but it is the same God who inspires them all in every one. To each is given the manifestation of the Spirit for the common good. To one is given through the Spirit the utterance of wisdom, and to another the utterance of knowledge according to the same Spirit, to another faith by the same Spirit, to another gifts of healing by the one Spirit, to another the working of miracles, to another prophecy, to another the ability to distinguish between spirits, to another various kinds of tongues, to another the interpretation of tongues. All these are inspired by one and the same Spirit, who apportions to each one individually as he wills" (1 Corinthians 12:4-11).

Paul goes on to explain that each member of the church is like a part of the body, each having its own function, and each important to the functioning of the whole. But he does recognize, as he points out in 1 Corinthians 12:28, that certain gifts are greater than others, and he regards the ministry of the prophet second only to that of the apostle.

Yet Paul emphasizes that none of the spiritual gifts

is worth anything to the person who exercises it unless that person has *agape*, the Greek word for unconditional, unselfish love. Prophecies will cease and tongues will become silent, he declares, but love, *agape*, never fails.

Paul is not suggesting that the gifts of the Spirit be ignored, but that *agape* govern their use. In fact, he encourages his followers to seek both *agape* and the charismatic gifts. The Corinthians were apparently highly impressed with the spiritual gift of speaking in tongues — that is, praying or praising God with sounds other than intelligible words. Paul encouraged speaking in tongues, but he stressed that he regarded prophecy as a higher gift: "Make love your aim, and earnestly desire the spiritual gifts, especially that you may prophesy. For one who speaks in a tongue speaks not to men but to God; for no one understands him, but he utters mysteries in the Spirit. On the other hand, he who prophesies speaks to men for their upbuilding and encouragement and consolation. He who speaks in a tongue edifies himself, but he who prophesies edifies the church. Now I want you all to speak in tongues, but even more to prophesy" (1 Corinthians 14:1-5).

In similar fashion, Paul urges Christians who speak in tongues to "pray for the gift of interpretation" so that others may understand. Otherwise, says Paul, ". . . you may give thanks well enough, but the other man is not edified. I thank God that I speak in tongues more than you all; nevertheless, in church I would rather speak five words with my mind, in order to instruct others, than ten thousand words in a tongue" (1 Corinthians 14:17-19).

Paul also insists that order should be maintained during church assemblies by seeing that prophecies are delivered one at a time.

For Paul, prophecy was not an occult phenomenon that issued from a trance state but a truth revealed to persons whose hearts were open to receive it. In urging the Corinthians to prophesy in an orderly manner, Paul reveals his understanding that prophecy doesn't simply come forth of its own accord. "The spirits of the prophets are under their prophets' control, since God is a God, not of confusion, but of peace" (1 Corinthians 14:32-33).

As much as he urged Christians to seek the gift of prophecy, Paul did not pretend that prophecy was infallible. "Let no more than two or three prophets speak, and let the rest judge the worth of what they say," he declares (see 1 Corinthians 14:29).

Paul saw prophecy as a gift given by God for the purpose of building up the church. The prophet, he says, "speaks to men for their upbuilding, their encouragement, their consolation" (1 Corinthians 14:3) and, in doing so, strengthens the body of Christ. And he was aware of the power of prophecy to directly penetrate the hearts of unbelievers. He declared that if an unbeliever should enter a gathering of Christians "while all are uttering prophecy, he will be taken to task by all and called to account by all, and the secret of his heart will be laid bare. Falling prostrate, he will worship God, crying out, 'God is truly among you' " (1 Corinthians 14:24-25).

To Paul, prophets were leaders of the church. His high regard for those who exercised this gift is explicitly

stated in his First Letter to the Corinthians: "God has
set up in the church first apostles; second prophets; third
teachers; then miracle workers, healers, assistants,
administrators, and those who speak in tongues"
(1 Corinthians 12:28).

And so it was in the first century. The followers of
Christ, instead of falling apart after the death of Jesus,
grasped the reality of the resurrection. Empowered by
the Holy Spirit, they discovered new gifts and learned
how to use them. Through the use of these gifts, including
the gift of prophecy, the church grew and its members
began spreading the Good News throughout the world.

CHAPTER SIX

True and False Prophecy in the Early Church

In A.D. 135, a journeying Christian named Justin arrived in the seaport city of Ephesus in Asia Minor and spent several days there waiting for a ship.

He was a well-educated man who wore the pallium, or cloak, of a philosopher, and one day as he walked through the streets of the city he was approached by another man who wanted to talk to him. The other man was a Jew named Trypho, a refugee from Palestine who had fled from the war that was raging between Jewish rebels and the Roman forces. Noticing that Justin wore the insignia of a philosopher, Trypho asked Justin to explain his philosophy. But Justin was not merely a philosopher, he was also a devout Christian.

Justin and Trypho talked for most of the next two days and Justin later wrote down the major points of their conversation. He called it *Dialogue with Trypho* and it has since become recognized as a second-century classic and a masterful defense of the Christian faith.

At one point in the *Dialogue*, Justin makes it clear that prophecy was not only an accepted feature of Christian worship in his time but that he considered it to be a continuation of the prophetic traditions of Judaism. At another point in the *Dialogue*, he tells Trypho, "From the fact that even to this day the gifts of prophecy exist among us Christians, you should realize that the gifts which had resided among your people have now been transferred to us."[1]

Justin, who was later beheaded for his writings (in which he vigorously defended the Christian faith), is known today as Saint Justin Martyr. He is one of several early Christian theologians whose writings indicate that the gift of prophecy was still normal and pervasive among Christians a full century after the death and resurrection of Jesus.

In Justin's time, the church had not yet defined much of its official dogma and the leading Christian thinkers of the day devoted themselves to exploring and working out the theological problems posed by the teaching of Christ and the apostles.

Some of the official teachings of the church that we now take for granted existed side by side with doctrines that were later defined as heretical. Justin, for instance, believed as the church has always taught, that Jesus was born of a virgin, but he also believed in an imminent return of Christ, to be followed by the "millennium," literally, a thousand-year reign of Christ on earth. The millennialist doctrine and some of the other doctrines promoted by early theologians were later defined as heresy, but there is no question that Christians like Justin, despite their occasional errors, were faithful promoters of the Gospel. He and many others, the movers and shakers of the early church, were later canonized. Justin and a number of his fellow theologians are now called the "fathers of the church."

The fathers of the church sometimes disagreed with one another on theological matters and it is probable that some of them diasgreed on when and how the gift of prophecy should be exercised in the church. The prophetic gift was probably more prevalent in some communities than in others, but early Christian literature, including the New Testament and the works of the church fathers, leaves no doubt that prophecy was a feature of first-century Christian life.

Some of the writings of early Christians contain teachings about prophecy and some contain examples of prophecy itself.

The Book of Revelation, the last book of the New Testament, contains prophetic oracles. So does the *Shepherd of Hermas*, a Christian exhortation to penance written by an anonymous second-century author. Both of these apocalyptic works contain prophetic messages, although it is not certain where they originated. Perhaps some of them were originally spoken by early Christian prophets or perhaps they originated in the authors' own dreams, visions, or insights.

Among the lesser known prophetic writings of the early church are the "Odes of Solomon," a collection of forty-two Christian hymns written in Syriac by a single author in the first quarter of the second century. The hymns are prophetic in tone and structure and some of them contain words attributed to Christ speaking through the author. At least one of the odes contains a prophecy declaring that prophecy is indeed a way in which Jesus speaks to his church: "Then I arose and am with them, / And will speak by their mouths."

Another tells of being inspired through visions granted by the Holy Spirit: "I rested on the Spirit of the Lord / And She lifted me up to heaven; / And caused me to stand on my feet in the Lord's high place, / Before His perfection and His glory, / Where I continued glorifying (Him) by the composition of his Odes" (Ode 36).

The "Odes of Solomon," of course, do not speak with the same kind of authority that the Bible does. In fact, many Christian scholars have not taken the odes very seriously because they are associated with heretical views. Nevertheless, they were written by second-century Christians and indicate that at least in some Christian circles prophetic hymns were accepted and used.

In addition to these texts containing written forms of prophecy, there are other Christian writings that affirm the continuing use of the prophetic gift. Saint Irenaeus, who lived in the second half of the second century, wrote,

"We have heard speaking in the church many brethren who possess the prophetic charisma; they speak by the Spirit in all languages and they reveal men's secrets."

Another early Christian document, the *Didache* (rhymes with "hid a key") sheds further light on the role of prophecy in the early church. The *Didache*, also called *The Teaching of the Twelve Apostles*, is an important collection of teachings and instructions believed to have been written during the second century. Among other things, it prescribes prayers of thanksgiving to be used after the completion of the Eucharist. Most of the worshipers were to use a rote prayer, but the *Didache* declares that "prophets" should be allowed "to render thanks as they desire."[2]

The idea seems to be that prophets, blessed with the ability to speak as the Spirit moves them, should not be hampered in the exercise of their gift as a means of thanksgiving.

As mentioned earlier, the New Testament shows that prophecy sometimes guided and directed early Christians in their decisions and actions. There are other nonbiblical sources that show the same thing.

Eusebius of Caesarea wrote that during the siege of Jerusalem which led to the destruction of the temple in A.D. 70, the Christian community there received a revelatory message instructing its members to flee the city. He stated that the command was given in an oracle.

Saint Ignatius of Antioch, who was martyred in Rome in the first half of the second century, once claimed in a letter that he had spoken in prophecy to the church at Philadelphia, urging the community to heed its leaders. He later wrote to the Philadelphians, reminding them of that occasion: "I cried out while I was with you, I spoke with a great voice, with the voice of God: To the bishop give heed, and to the presbytery, and to the deacons.

"But some suspected that I said these things because I already knew of the division caused by certain people. But he is my witness in whom I am bound that I learned nothing from any human being, but the Spirit was proclaiming by speaking in this manner:

"Apart from the bishop do nothing;

"Guard your flesh as the temple of God;

"Love unity;

"Flee divisions;

"Be imitators of Jesus Christ as he was of the Father!"[3]

The scene, as Ignatius describes it, is reminiscent of the biblical teaching in which Saint Paul declares in 1 Corinthians 14:25 that prophecy has the ability to disclose the secrets of the human heart.

The *Shepherd of Hermas* not only acknowledges the exercise of the prophetic gift but provides a brief theological explanation of how God uses it to address a community of believers: "When a man who has the Divine Spirit enters a gathering of just men who have faith in God's spirit, and an entreaty is addressed to God by such a gathering, at that moment the angel of the prophetic spirit, who is attached to this man, fills him and in the fullness of the Holy Spirit he speaks to the gathering in accordance with the Lord's wishes. In this manner, then, the spirit of the Deity will be made clear.

This, then, is the power of the Lord's divine spirit."[4]

Certain early Christian texts indicate that some of the Christian communities had prophets in their midst while others did not. The *Didache* suggests that a community's prophets are teachers whose material needs should be provided by the community. "Accordingly," it urges, "take all the first fruits of the winepress and of the harvest, of the cattle and of the sheep, and give them to the prophets, for they are your high priests. But if you have not a prophet, give it to the poor." The prophets were also to be given silver, clothing, bread, and oil.[5]

There were also prophets who traveled and visited communities other than their own. They, too, were to be fed, but the *Didache* adds a word of caution about them. It recognized that not everyone who claims to be a prophet actually speaks the word of God.

The problem of differentiating between true and false prophecy was as real to the early Christians as it had been among the Jews of the Old Testament.

Jesus himself had warned that in the last days false prophets would arise and the early church, which expected his imminent return, took the warning seriously. In his *Dialogue*, Justin declares to Trypho, "He predicted that we would be martyred and hated because of his name, and that many false prophets and false Christs would start preaching in his name and would mislead many; and this has actually happened."

The New Testament and other Christian writings recognized the problem and taught early Christians how to deal with it. These early texts frequently express

the understanding that the validity of prophecy is
determined by the spirit that inspires it.

The Second Letter of Peter declares, "Prophecy has
never been put forward by man's willing it. It is rather
that men impelled by the Holy Spirit have spoken under
God's influence" (2 Peter 1:21). The letter goes on to say
that false prophets and teachers, motivated not by God
but by greed and lust, would arise among the members of
the church and would lead Christians astray.

Identifying the spirit behind the prophecy required
the ability to recognize delusion as well as deceit. Just
because a prophet believed he was speaking the word of
God did not guarantee that this was so.

The First Letter of John gives this prescription for
judging prophecy: "Beloved, / do not trust every spirit, /
but put the spirits to a test / to see if they belong to God, /
because many false prophets have appeared in the world.
/ This is how you can recognize God's Spirit: / every
spirit that acknowledges Jesus Christ come in the flesh /
belongs to God, / while every spirit that fails to
acknowledge him / does not belong to God" (1 John
4:1-3).

Paul gave a similar prescription when he wrote to
the Corinthians, telling them that "nobody who speaks in
the Spirit of God ever says, 'Cursed be Jesus.' And no one
can say: 'Jesus is Lord,' except in the Holy Spirit"
(1 Corinthians 12:3).

Paul and John are both declaring that the Spirit of
God always speaks in harmony with the truth revealed in
the birth, death, resurrection, and redemptive power of
the man-God, Jesus. Jesus, in other words, is the

revelation of truth by which all teaching and prophecy must be measured.

The *Didache*, like the writings of John and Paul, warned against listening to prophets who spoke a false doctrine, but it also emphasized the need to consider the behavior as well as the words of the prophet. It cautions that "not everyone who speaks in the spirit is a prophet, but only if he follows the conduct of the Lord. Accordingly, from their conduct, the false prophet and the true prophet will be known."[6]

One of the attributes of a false prophet, according to the *Didache*, was a tendency to take advantage of a community's generosity or to ask for money. Prophets and teachers were to be respected; but if they hung around, accepting food, drink, and money, they were to be sent packing. A day or two was as long as a true prophet would accept such hospitality. "But if he stays for three, he is a false prophet," the *Didache* declares.[7] The *Didache* echoes the words of Jesus himself who declared that Christians would be able to know false prophets "by their deeds" (Matthew 7:16).

The *Shepherd of Hermas* makes another distinction between listening to the word of God and "consulting" false prophets. "For no spirit granted by God has to be consulted," the document declares. "It speaks everything with the Godhead's power, because it is from above, from the power of the Divine Spirit. But the spirit that is consulted and speaks according to the desires of men is earthly and weak, without any power. Besides, it does not speak at all, unless it be consulted."

According to the *Shepherd of Hermas* a prophet

who has the "Divine Spirit" is meek, calm, and humble. "He abstains from all wickedness and vain desires of this world, and considers that he is inferior to all men. He does not give answers to questions, either, nor does he speak by himself (neither does the Holy Spirit speak when a man wishes Him to speak), but he speaks when God wishes him to speak."

The ability of early Christians to discern the spirit behind a prophecy wasn't entirely a matter of using good judgment and human wisdom. It also depended on God-given "power to distinguish one spirit from another," explicitly named by Saint Paul as one of the gifts of the Holy Spirit, along with prophecy, wisdom, faith, the power to express knowledge, the gift of healing, miraculous powers, the gift of tongues, and the ability to interpret what is spoken in tongues (see 1 Corinthians 12:10).

Throughout most of the first and second centuries, prophecy continued to be an accepted part of the Christian life, although its importance began to diminish. Increasingly, the responsibility for teaching was exercised by the bishops as the successors of the apostles. And as the teaching authority of the bishops increased, the authority of the prophets correspondingly decreased. Around the end of the second century, a major crisis developed over prophecy and its use in the church. The crisis revolved around a group of Christians who put prophecy at the very center of their lives. They not only prophesied but believed that their prophecies should guide the entire church. Their leader was a man named Montanus.

Montanus, a pagan at birth, came from the Grecian territory of Phrygia, an area where warfare and persecution had raged intensely during the second century. He became a follower of Christ and, shortly after his baptism, the leader of a second-century charismatic movement whose prophets declared that the wars and persecutions of their age were signs of the imminent return of the Lord Jesus.

In other parts of the church, prophecy and other charismatic gifts may have begun to wane but not among Montanus and his followers. Sometimes the Montanist prophets spoke in the first person in the voice of the Trinity. In one such oracle, for instance, Montanus is quoted as declaring, "I am the Father and the Son and the Holy Spirit." He was not claiming to be God, but was claiming that God was speaking through him. In early Christianity, prophecy in this form was unusual but not necessarily unique.

In most ways, the beliefs and practices of Montanism were in harmony with the rest of the early church. The difference was the emphasis that Montanists placed on the importance of prophecy and their curious beliefs concerning the imminent establishment of the "New Jerusalem."

Montanus and two of his followers, Priscilla and Maximilla, were the chief prophets of the sect. They called their sect the "New Prophecy," but their Christian critics called it the "Phrygian Heresy." The Montanists claimed that the coming of Christ would be ushered in by the descent of the New Jerusalem from heaven, a belief based on a literal interpretation of

Revelation 21:2. Based on oracles spoken by their
prophets, they expected the heavenly city to descend
near a place called Pepuza. There, Jesus would return to
reign for a thousand years.

The sect and its beliefs quickly spread throughout the
Greco-Roman world. Even though the New Jerusalem
failed to appear, Montanism continued to influence
Christians for several centuries, in spite of the opposition
of several popes.

A couple of centuries later, Eusebius described
Montanism as the work of the devil. Nevertheless, in its
own time it had been a powerful movement within the
church. Even though it had been denounced as heresy by
some of the fathers of the church, it had been applauded
by others, including the brilliant third-century theologian
Tertullian, who actually became a Montanist and wrote
enthusiastically, "There is among us a sister who has
been favored with wonderful gifts of revelation which she
experiences in an ecstasy of the spirit during the sacred
ceremonies on the Lord's day. She converses with the
angels and, sometimes, with the Lord Himself. She
perceives hidden mysteries and has the power of reading
the hearts of men and of prescribing remedies for such as
need them."[8]

Eusebius and others have attempted to paint
Montanus and his followers as pagans, but they were not.
They were a misguided Christian sect — a second-
century charismatic renewal movement which made the
mistake of embracing revelations that went beyond the
teaching of Christ and the apostles.

The Montanist heresy is generally regarded by

scholars as a turning point in the church's attitude toward the gift of prophecy. Certainly, in the years that followed, prophets who exercised this gift were no longer honored in the manner that Saint Paul had honored them — as leaders who shared authority with the apostles.

Origen, a third-century Christian theologian from Egypt, observed that prophecy and other charismatic gifts had diminished in the church but declared, "There are still traces of (the Holy Spirit's) presence in a few."

The gift of prophecy did not disappear from the church, but it was greatly diminished. Over the centuries, there have been mystics, saints, and martyrs who have heard and spoken God's word, but their prophecies (or "revelations," as the church preferred to call them) were seen as manifestations of exceptional holiness rather than as a gift that any spirit-filled Christian believer might receive.

CHAPTER SEVEN

Prophecy Through the Centuries

After witnessing the ability of false prophecy to lead the faithful astray, the church became much more guarded in its acceptance of prophecy.

It became clear that if prophecy was to function at all, there would have to be people in the church who had not only the ability to discern true prophecy but the authority to control it. As a result, the authority of church prophets was greatly diminished.

Saint Paul had considered the prophets of the early church — along with the apostles — to be the leaders of the church.

In his Letter to the Ephesians, Paul refers to the prophets and apostles together as the foundation of the church and says both received the full Revelation of Christ (Ephesians 2:20). But the prophets of the church didn't continue to hold strong positions of authority. Increasingly, the leadership of the church was exercised by the successors of the apostles — the bishops.

Some scholars declare that prophecy ceased to exist in the church. Biblical scholar John L. McKenzie declares in his *Dictionary of the Bible* that "prophecy does not appear after New Testament times; as Old Testament prophecy yielded to the scribe, so New Testament prophecy was submerged in the development of the hierarchical offices." McKenzie declares that after the first century, prophecy was claimed almost exclusively by heretical sects (like the Montanists).

Prophecy did cease to exist in the way that it existed in Paul's time. And yet there were still persons within the church through whom God continued to reveal his word.

The decline in prophecy was part of a general decline in the use of the gifts of the Holy Spirit. The writers of the New Testament described many instances of healing, miracles, speaking in tongues, and similar events; but with the passage of time, the manifestation of such gifts became rare.

In the beginning, the church had been a small apocalyptic Jewish sect consumed by the knowledge of Jesus as Savior and Lord. Its members expected his imminent return and were willing to die, if necessary, to remain faithful until he came. Throughout the first two centuries, Christians faced wave after wave of persecutions. In those days, Christians lived with and accepted the possibility that their faith might cost them their lives. The church was small, but it was on fire. It was not a church of lukewarm Christians but a church whose members were passionately responsive to the Gospel and filled with a faith that invited God to manifest himself in marvelous ways.

This continued to be so throughout the first and second centuries. But after the emperor Constantine officially put an end to the persecution of Christians in 313, the church began to attract a much wider variety of believers. The ordinary Christian life no longer included a call to martyrdom. In fact, in a relatively short time, Christianity became the official religion of the Roman Empire. This acceptance made the church a tamer place than it had been. There still were, of course, individuals for whom Jesus was the only thing that mattered, believers who insisted on devoting themselves wholeheartedly to Christ and the Good News. Holy men and women of that sort began setting up communities in the deserts of Egypt to devote themselves to prayer, fasting, penance, and the worship of God. As they did so, they were establishing the roots of the monastic tradition in the church.

Among such individuals, many charismatic gifts, including the ability to hear and speak God's word, continued. During the Middle Ages, the monastic tradition flourished, producing many holy men and women known for their devotion to God and for their spiritual gifts. Throughout the Middle Ages, the word "prophecy" was rarely used to describe such gifts, however. Theologians spoke instead of "revelations" received by holy individuals. In fact, such revelations included not only prophetic messages but dreams, visions, and ecstatic experiences.

Saint Augustine, the bishop of Hippo (a Mediterranean port city in what is now Algeria), was an important theologian of the fourth and fifth centuries — a man whose writings have made a lasting impact on the church, shaping Catholic thought from the early Middle Ages into the present time. By Augustine's time, the charismatic gifts had all but disappeared and he tended to be skeptical of those who claimed them. But toward the end of his life he grew in his acceptance of personal revelations and healing. He wrote about some revelations that he regarded as genuine — including those of his mother whom he said could discern true revelation from her own thoughts and dreams.

Toward the end of the Middle Ages, the thirteenth-century theologian Saint Thomas Aquinas wrote his monumental *Summa Theologica* and included in it a treatise on prophecy, in which he claimed that it was a gift for all ages. "There have never been lacking men having the spirit of prophecy," he wrote, "not in truth for developing a new doctrine of faith, but for directing human activity."

This observation of Thomas Aquinas on the purpose of prophecy is an important one and we shall examine it further in another chapter. At the time that Thomas was writing the *Summa*, the church in Europe was beginning to experience a controversial reappearance of prophetic gifts. Thomas witnessed the beginnings of a period in which the church in Europe abounded with prophets, both true and false.

One of the first of these was an abbot named Joachim of Fiore (or Floris), from a section of what is now Italy, who died at the beginning of the thirteenth century. He was both a visionary and a scholarly theologian with some controversial ideas about the nature of the Holy Trinity. Joachim, whose ideas were inspired, in part, by his own prophetic visions, believed that the world was divided into three ages, each of which corresponded to one of the persons of the Holy Trinity. He taught that the age of God the Son was drawing to a close and that the age of God the Holy Spirit was soon to begin. As a prophet, Joachim is said to have foretold the birth of two great preaching orders — the Franciscans and the Dominicans — that were soon to emerge in the church.

Joachim's views of the Trinity were complex and not easily understood, and some of his critics believed they were in error. But he was encouraged in his writing by several popes, including Lucius III, and his work was taken seriously by some of the best Catholic thinkers of his day. After his death, some of Joachim's admirers began to explore his work.

Joachim himself would probably have been horrified by the wild apocalyptic speculation of his would-be disciples. A half century after Joachim's death, an enthusiastic young friar named Gerardo of Borgo San Donnino, in 1254, wrote an interpretation of Joachim's major works, claiming that Joachim was a prophet who had predicted that the age of the Holy Spirit would begin in 1260. Gerardo predicted that in the new age the church would be abolished and the Old and New Testaments would be replaced by the writings of Joachim.

Gerardo was thrown into prison and his work condemned by the church. But the work of Joachim was not condemned and it helped to inspire a lively interest in apocalyptic speculation and prophecy. By this time, the church in the later Middle Ages was suffering from widespread corruption and some important new renewal movements. Prophecy became a means by which a number of holy men and women arose to call the church back to God. Saint Francis of Assisi, Saint Bridget (or Birgitta) of Sweden, Saint Catherine of Siena, and Saint Vincent Ferrer are some of the better known prophets of the thirteenth- through fifteenth-century church.

The prophetic gifts of Saint Catherine are particularly well-documented through her own writings and the writings of those who knew her.

Catherine manifested many remarkable gifts, including the charismatic gifts of prophecy and healing. Perhaps the most remarkable thing about Catherine was her intimate relationship with Jesus, who began appearing to her in visions when she was a small child. Throughout her life, she "conversed" with Jesus. She spoke to him and he spoke to her. Her book, *The Dialogue*, written as spiritual direction for her followers, is a collection of teachings revealed to her by God.

Throughout her life, the visions continued. Some of her prophecies were for the guidance of the entire church. Catherine believed that she was chosen and empowered by Jesus to help purify the church which, at that time, was torn by dissension, corruption, and power struggles. And despite the fact that she never had any formal education, her prophetic gifts enabled her to become an adviser even to the pope.

On the night of April 1, 1376, she experienced a major revelation that she later described in a letter to her friend and biographer Raymond of Capua.

"God revealed His mysteries to me and showed me His wonderful counsels in such a way that my soul no longer knew whether it was in the body, and I was filled with such abundant joy that my tongue has no power to express it," she wrote.

During the revelation, she said, Jesus appeared to her and declared, "I do as I did when I was here on earth and made a scourge of cords and drove out those who bought and sold in the temple. For I have made a scourge of men and with this scourge I drive out the unclean, covetous, miserly and proud peddlers who buy and sell the gifts of the Holy Spirit."

Based on this revelation, Catherine declared that the church would undergo a time of persecution and purification, followed by a period of glory that would bring salvation to many. This revelation was followed by a vision, during which Catherine says she "marvelled to see both Christians and infidels entering into the wound in the heart of Christ crucified, and I walked into the midst of them and entered into Christ sweet Jesus together with my father, Saint Dominic, and the Friend of my heart, John (her pet name for Raymond of Capua), and all my spiritual children. And then He laid the Cross upon my shoulder and placed the branch of olive in my hand, and said to me that I was to go out with it to all people. And He said to me: 'Go and tell them: behold I bring you tidings of great joy.' "[1]

Catherine's prophecy wasn't always based directly on such visions. She had an understanding of her time that seems to have been formed by wisdom and knowledge as well as by revelation. When the nearby city-state of Perugia rebelled against the pope, the news devastated Raymond, but Catherine told him, "You begin to weep too soon. Save your tears for a better occasion. That which you see now is only milk and honey compared to what is to come."

She went on to declare, "Today it is the laity who rebel against our sweet Christ on earth, but soon it will be the clergy who turn against him." In later years Raymond remembered these words of Catherine's and only then understood them to be a prophecy concerning the great schism that was to break upon the Church within a few short years.

Catherine frequently wrote to Pope Gregory XI advising him about the affairs of the church. Both he and his advisers wrote to her, too, seeking her counsel. In one letter she urged the Holy Father to forgive the rebellion of the city of Florence and welcome its citizens back into the church.

"Holiest sweet Babbo mine," she wrote, "I see no other way for us, and no other help in winning back your sheep, which have left the fold of Holy Church in rebellion, not obedient nor subject to you, their father. . . . I ask you, Father, to show them mercy. Do not regard the ignorance and pride of your sons. . . .

"I tell you, sweet Christ on earth, on behalf of Christ in Heaven, that if you do thus, without any strife or tempest, they will all come, grieving for the wrong they have done, and will put their heads in your bosom. Then you will rejoice, and we shall rejoice, because by love you have restored the wandering sheep to the fold of Holy Church."[2]

Catherine was confident that she knew God's will and that the pope needed to hear it from her. Today, we stand in awe that this woman, who lived in an age when women's roles were limited mainly to prayer or motherhood, would dare to speak in such a bold manner. Yet she was neither the first nor the last woman of the Middle Ages who delivered prophecies to a pope.

Her immediate predecessor in this role was Saint Bridget of Sweden, a mystic with strong opinions on the politics and policies of the church, and the courage to speak them out boldly to the popes. Bridget's messages were austere and harshly worded warnings about the doom that would descend on the church unless the pope acted promptly. Catherine addressed the same concerns and issued similar calls to action, but her letters, in contrast to Bridget's doleful messages, were warm and earthy, stressing reconciliation rather than judgment.

During the period when the papacy had moved to Avignon, Catherine became a personal friend of Pope Gregory and consistently urged him to return to Rome. But the Holy Father was torn by factional disputes within the church. Once, he asked Catherine, as he had on previous occasions, what she would do if she were in his position.

Her reply seems to have been based on supernatural knowledge of the pope's heart: "Who knows what ought to be done better than your Holiness, who has long since made a vow to God to return to Rome?"[3]

Gregory was astonished because Catherine had read his heart and found there a secret promise he had made many years ago. He believed that Catherine's knowledge was a sign from God, confirming his determination to restore the papacy to Rome. But Catherine's prophecies weren't limited to affairs of state. On other occasions, Catherine's friends and acquaintances saw her use prophetic gifts simply to bring individuals closer to God.

One such occasion occurred when two scholarly theologians tried to expose her as a pious but ignorant religious fanatic. Catherine at that time was living in her parents' home in Siena, and a small group of friends used to spend their evenings there, praying with Catherine and listening to her as she talked to them about God. The two theologians, Brother Gabriel of Volterra and Father John Tantucci, were convinced that she was leading her friends astray with false teaching.

One evening, while Catherine and her friends were praying in her small room, the two learned men set out from a nearby village to visit her and discredit her. One of Catherine's friends, Father Francesco Malavolti, who was present that night, later wrote about what happened.

He says that in the midst of a discourse, Catherine stopped talking suddenly and began to pray with great fervor, her face aglow with love. After a time she turned

her attention again to her friends. She smiled gently,
saying, "Soon you will see two great fish caught in a
net." Her friends, puzzled, were on the verge of asking
her what she was talking about when a servant
announced that Brother Gabriel and Father Tantucci
were at the door asking permission to see Catherine.

The two men were ushered in and began posing
questions designed to expose Catherine's lack of
understanding. When they finished and it was time for
her to respond, she asked vehemently: "How can you
begin to understand anything that pertains to the
kingdom of God? You who live only for the world, and
seek to be honored by men and not by God? Your great
learning is no help to you or to others. It only harms you
because you seek the shell and not the core!" Turning
toward Brother Gabriel she said, "How can you, a son of
Saint Francis, dare to live the way you do?"

Brother Gabriel, who had transformed his monastic
cell into a luxurious room, was suddenly exposed and
shamed by this simple, uneducated woman who could
read his heart. "For the sake of Jesus Christ crucified,"
she admonished him, "do not live this way any longer!"[4]

The two men who had come to destroy her credibility
instead became her disciples.

Catherine's prophetic gifts were extraordinary, but
she was not infallible. Like other prophets of her century,
she sometimes "foretold" events that never came to
pass. For one thing, she promoted and campaigned for a
new crusade, declared that it was God's will, and
prophesied great success for it. Eventually, she

convinced the pope. The crusade was launched, but it was a dismal failure.

Catherine wasn't the only prophetic saint of the Middle Ages who made mistakes. Bernard of Clairvaux similarly prophesied success for an unsuccessful crusade. And Pope Saint Gregory VII publicly prophesied in 1080 that the German emperor Henry would be dead or deposed within a year. As it turned out, Henry's reign outlasted Gregory's by twenty-one years.

Another great saint of the late Middle Ages was Saint Vincent Ferrer, whose powerful gift of preaching led to the repentance and conversion of thousands. Vincent is said to have worked many miracles and to have spoken many prophecies. Vincent is a canonized saint whose preaching and holiness are beyond dispute, but he erred in attempting to specify a timetable for the end of the world — a mistake which has been repeated countless times throughout the history of Christianity. Beginning in 1398, Vincent preached that the end of the world was at hand. He declared that the antichrist, although not identified, was already born and living among the people of that age. Eventually, his prophecy was realized, at least in part, not by the end of the world, but by the end of Saint Vincent Ferrer's world. He died in 1419.

The fourteenth century had its share, too, of false prophets among heretical Franciscan sects that saw themselves as the true guardians of the faith. Members of a Franciscan sect known as the Fraticelli went so far as to depict Pope John XXII as the antichrist. Finally, in reaction against such spiritual enthusiasm, the pope condemned the Fraticelli.

Another kind of prophecy began to appear in Europe soon after the Reformation. Martin Luther himself did not encourage the use of prophetic gifts and was distrustful of those who did. Aware of the prophetic excesses of the Middle Ages, Luther and other Protestant reformers rejected various forms of prophecy on the grounds that Scripture was the only trustworthy source of revelation. But in 1520, only three years after Luther had nailed his theses to the door of the cathedral at Wittenberg, the first of many prophetic sects emerged among the Protestants through the prophets of a religious movement known as Anabaptists.

The sect rejected infant baptism and preached simplicity and separation of church and state. Luther disowned the Anabaptists, not only because they rejected the baptism of infants, but even more because of their attitude toward prophecy. They believed that the gift of prophecy was intended by God for all ages. They recognized the authority of Scripture but believed that Scripture was worthless unless interpreted by persons under the inspiration of the Holy Spirit. To the Anabaptists, the break from Catholicism offered an opportunity to rediscover the gift of prophecy that had guided the church in the first century.

And prophesy they did. Philipp Melanchthon, a German reformer, wrote in the sixteenth century that the Anabaptists had declared to him "that they are positively sent by God to teach; that they have familiar conferences with God, that they can foretell events; and, to be brief, that they are on a footing with prophets and apostles." (Among the events they predicted was the "second coming of Christ" in 1533.)

Melanchthon had mixed feelings about these claims. "I cannot describe how I am moved by these lofty pretensions," he wrote. "I see strong reasons for not despising the men; for it is clear to me that there is in them something more than a human spirit; but whether the spirit be of God or not, none except Martin [Luther] can easily judge."[5]

Like so many other prophetic movements since the time of the Montanists, the Anabaptists were convinced that the existing world order was drawing to a close. One of their prophets, Melchior Hoffman, announced that Christ would return in 1533, the fifteen hundredth anniversary of the death and resurrection of Jesus.

The Anabaptists were zealous evangelists whose converts gathered in the city of Munster, which became a renegade fortress city, besieged by the forces of the Reformation. When Munster fell in 1535, the movement was crushed, but the beliefs of the Anabaptists continued to influence other Protestant groups like the early Quakers and the French Huguenots.

The Huguenots were a Protestant group who faced severe persecution by the rulers of France in the 1680s. During the course of the persecution, some of the Huguenots in southern France began to see apparitions, to speak in tongues, and to prophesy. Not surprisingly, their prophecies had a marked anti-Catholic tone. In 1700, an unusual movement began in which Huguenot children, some as young as three years old, entered ecstatic states and prophesied. The continued persecution of the Huguenots scattered the "French prophets," as they were called, throughout Europe.

About a century later, new manifestations of the gifts of the Spirit began to appear in other parts of the world. In 1830, in Glasgow, Scotland, a Presbyterian minister named Edward Irving became convinced through his study of the Bible that the end of the world was imminent. Believing that the Second Coming would be preceded by a new outpouring of charismatic gifts, he prayed openly for a return of the gifts of Pentecost. Before long, people in Irving's congregation were soon prophesying and speaking in tongues. When the Presbyterian church relieved him of his ministry, Irving and his followers founded the "Catholic Apostolic Church."

It wasn't long before similar things were happening in America. After the Civil War, "Holiness" churches (an offshoot of Methodism) preached a "second blessing" — a personal religious experience that was sought by those who were already baptized. Five persons, including a Holiness minister named R.B. Swan, claimed to have received the gift of tongues in Providence, Rhode Island, in 1875.

But it wasn't until the beginning of this century that the Pentecostal movement bloomed. In the last days of 1900, a Holiness minister named Charles Fox Parham, who headed the Bethel Bible College in Topeka, assigned his students to study the references in the New Testament to "baptism in the Holy Spirit" and the phenomenon of speaking in tongues. On New Year's eve, as Parham prayed over one of his students so that she might receive the Holy Spirit, the student began to speak in tongues.

Within a month, most of the other students had experienced a "Spirit baptism" and had spoken in "other tongues."

That was the beginning of the modern Pentecostal movement. After about two years, it began to grow rapidly, spreading to many parts of the world. But those who spoke in tongues and prophesied soon found that such behavior wasn't welcomed in the Protestant churches to which they belonged. In most cases, the tongues speakers were forced to either abandon their newly acquired gift or to leave their churches. As a result, the new Pentecostals began forming their own church bodies. The Pentecostal movement today claims several million members in America and millions more in other parts of the world.

The antagonism of other churches toward the Pentecostals began to wane in the middle of the twentieth century. Eventually members of other denominations began to listen to the Pentecostals who were claiming that "baptism in the Holy Spirit" was as valid in the twentieth century as it was in the first.

In 1960, in Van Nuys, California, an Episcopalian rector by the name of Dennis J. Bennett experienced baptism in the Holy Spirit and began ministering to a few others in his parish who sought it. But when he told the rest of the parish what had been happening, he was asked to resign. The incident, which received national publicity, made it clear that charismatic gifts in the

twentieth century were not the exclusive property of
Pentecostals.

By 1970, a new ecumenical charismatic movement
had emerged in which Episcopalians, Baptists,
Lutherans, Congregationalists, Methodists,
Presbyterians, Catholics, and others were reviving the
gift of prophecy within their own churches.

•

CHAPTER EIGHT

•

Charismatic Prophecy: A Pipeline to God?

•

Looking back, it appears that the twentieth-century Roman Catholic Church was moving toward a charismatic renewal even before it happened.

By the middle of the 1960s, many Catholics, inspired by Vatican II, were seeking a renewal of their commitment to God and the church. The Cursillo movement was introducing many of these Catholics to a deeper spiritual relationship with the Lord than they had previously known.

At the same time, in the mainline Protestant churches, the neo-Pentecostal movement

was spreading rapidly. During the mid-sixties, a book
called *The Cross and the Switchblade*, by Pentecostal
minister David Wilkerson, was having a tremendous
impact on Christians of all denominations. The book
described, in a readable and credible way, how
Wilkerson overcame nearly insurmountable obstacles to
minister successfully to street gangs in New York simply
by listening to the Lord, obeying him, and calling on him
for help. For people who had never been involved with
the Pentecostals, the most striking aspect of Wilkerson's
story was the matter-of-fact way in which the minister
received divine guidance. Wilkerson's relationship with
God was one in which God spoke and Wilkerson listened.
He didn't hear voices spoken aloud but heard them in his
heart and mind. He trusted that this direction was from
God and acted on it — with impressive results.

Wilkerson's book found a wide readership. In the
ecumenical atmosphere that followed Vatican II, the
Catholic Church and the neo-Pentecostal movement
began to discover each other. Among those who read and
were influenced by Wilkerson's book were two Catholic
theology professors at Duquesne University in
Pittsburgh. After being prayed over by some
Episcopalian neo-Pentecostals, the two professors
experienced what Pentecostals call "baptism of the Holy
Spirit."

The Catholic charismatic renewal dates its
beginnings to the late 1960s. There may have been
isolated earlier instances in which Catholics had begun to
share in the Pentecostal experience, but the event that
launched the movement into the Catholic Church

occurred at Duquesne University early in 1967. Two professors and a small group of Catholic students began asking the Lord to let them experience what their Pentecostal brothers and sisters called "baptism in the Holy Spirit." On February 17, the professors and a group of student members of a Christian study-and-action group gathered for a weekend retreat. In preparation for the retreat, the professors asked the students to read the Acts of the Apostles. During the course of the weekend, the students prayed, praised God, and yielded themselves to Christ, promising to love and serve him and asking him to fill them with the Holy Spirit.

Before the weekend was over, they had experienced the Lord's power and felt his love. Many of them prophesied and spoke in tongues. Word of what had happened spread rapidly among other Catholics seeking "baptism in the Holy Spirit," and by the end of that year, similar experiences had occurred at the University of Notre Dame and elsewhere.

Many "Catholic Pentecostals," as they called themselves at first, declared their belief that God was bringing about the "new Pentecost" that Pope John had prayed for. The pope didn't live to see it happen, but before the end of the 1960s, thousands of Catholics throughout the world were speaking in tongues, prophesying, and claiming to have discovered a deep, personal relationship with God. By 1985, an estimated seven and a half million Catholics had shared what they insisted was the experience of Pentecost in their own lives.

The Catholic hierarchy, at first, was wary of the new

movement. Although the Catholic Pentecostals embraced traditional Catholic doctrine, the church was taken by surprise by this sudden grassroots charismatic explosion. Catholic doctrine didn't forbid prophecy or speaking in tongues, but these were certainly not ordinary manifestations of Catholicism as it had been practiced in recent centuries. In at least one diocese, church officials forbade Catholics to speak in tongues at prayer meetings. In most places, however, the movement was cautiously tolerated and it soon became clear that most Catholic charismatics were remaining loyal to their church. In fact, many of them became more devout in their practice of Catholic devotions and Mass attendance.

The practice of speaking in tongues attracted much attention and was frequently ridiculed by noncharismatic Catholics, but the gift of prophecy seemed to flourish without attracting much attention. On the surface, speaking in tongues seems bizarre and extreme; in reality, the gift of prophecy, in which the individual Christian actually claims to be speaking for God is the more radical and powerful gift. Saint Paul was aware of this, but even after two decades of charismatic renewal, most Catholics hardly seem aware that many of their fellow churchgoers claim to hear God himself talking to them.

In the late 1960s and early 1970s, a few bishops sought to suppress the use of charismatic gifts. At least one diocese forbade speaking in tongues and the laying on of hands at charismatic prayer meetings. Oddly, the only charismatic gift not forbidden was prophecy and that, apparently, was an oversight on the part of diocesan officials. In obedience to the church, the prayer group members accepted the regulations. They didn't speak in tongues or lay hands on the people they prayed for, but for the first time, some of them began to prophesy. Among the prophecies spoken were these: "Bear in all patience what has happened to you. Obey those I have put over you. See the care I have for my flock," and "Fear not, for the wonders I have worked among you shall not cease."[1]

Eventually, the hierarchy accepted the movement and many bishops even encouraged it. In 1975, when ten thousand Catholics gathered in Rome for the Third International Conference of the Catholic Charismatic Renewal, Pope Paul VI gave the movement his blessing, calling it "a chance for the church and the world."

In 1981, Pope John Paul II said that the hopes expressed by Paul VI had been borne out. "The church has seen the fruits of your devotion to prayer in a deepened commitment to holiness of life and love for the word of God," he told movement leaders.

The difference between charismatic and noncharismatic Catholics is not so much a difference in beliefs but a difference in the way those beliefs are expressed. The only important difference, it seems to me, is that charismatics expect the Holy Spirit to distribute extraordinary gifts in the church today, just as he did in the church of the first century. A Catholic priest who has been active in charismatic renewal since the late 1960s once told me it should be a part of normal Christianity to have a "pipeline to God." By that, he meant that all Christians have received the Holy Spirit in baptism and, whether they realize it or not, have inherited a relationship with Jesus that God wants all his people to enjoy — a relationship in which God's word is more clearly perceived.

Many Catholics may be satisfied with the traditional devotions they grew up with, but charismatics believe that God wants to establish a close, personal relationship with each believer. Most Catholics, charismatic or not, would agree that they have a relationship with God and that God makes his will known in a variety of ways: through Scripture, through Holy Tradition, and through the teaching authority of the church. But charismatics and Pentecostals believe that God wants the relationship to be so intimate that he can speak through them just as he did through Moses, through Isaiah, and through the prophets of the early church.

The gift of prophecy, as it is manifested in the Catholic charismatic renewal, seeks to follow the model of the early church as described in the New Testament.

In some Catholic prayer groups, prophecy is more common than in others. But in almost every large, well-organized charismatic prayer community, prophecies are an accepted part of communal prayer, along with hymns, songs of praise, readings from Scripture, inspired teaching or preaching, and testimonies from people who have experienced God's love and power in their own lives.

It is a common misconception that prophecy means a foretelling of the future. Among Catholic charismatics, prophecy has other purposes, all of them aimed at increasing the love of the believers for God and one another. Charismatics see prophecy, as Saint Paul did, as a way of building up, encouraging, and consoling the members of the Church (1 Corinthians 14:3). Bruce Yocum, who is responsible for guiding the use of the gift of prophecy at The Word of God, a charismatic community in Ann Arbor, Michigan, declares that God gives the prophetic gift for four distinct purposes: (1) encouragement; (2) conviction, admonition, or correction; (3) inspiration; and (4) guidance.[2]

In my own fifteen years of participating in prayer meetings and charismatic conferences, I have heard many prophecies in which God promised joy, harmony, and love to those who love him, but I cannot recall a single prophecy that predicted a specific future event. This is not to say that God never reveals the future, but it is my own experience that he usually speaks for other purposes.

In the charismatic renewal, prophecies are delivered in the first person by ordinary people. At a prayer meeting, when a prophet uses the word "I," it doesn't refer to the prophet but to God. If Jim or Mary says, "My children, love one another even as my Father and I love you," those assembled understand that it is Jesus who speaks. If the prophet says, "Listen to my son (or daughter)," the members of the prayer group understand this to mean that God the Father is speaking.

To some people, it may seem ludicrous that Jim the mechanic or Mary the real-estate broker should presume to speak for God. In the Old Testament, prophets were extraordinary men and women whose lives and deeds separated them from the lives and deeds of ordinary people. But in the New Testament, any believer who has received the Holy Spirit is a potential prophet.

In the words of Saint Paul, "To each is given the manifestation of the Spirit for the common good" (1 Corinthians 12:7), and Paul lists some of the ways that the Spirit is manifested: wisdom, knowledge, faith, the gift of healing, the ability to work miracles, to distinguish one spirit from another, to speak in tongues, to interpret what is said in tongues, and to prophesy.

In the charismatic renewal today, men and women from all walks of life speak prophecies. "In my experience," says Father Michael Scanlan, a national charismatic leader, "everyone who has been baptized in the Holy Spirit can be guided in the use of the gift of prophecy."[3]

Although the ability to prophesy is seen as a gift which might be given to any baptized believer, the expression of the gift varies from person to person. Some people, says Yocum, actually seem to "hear" the words that God wants them to speak. Others receive a general sense of what the Lord wants to say and feel that God is calling them to express that message in the best words they can find. Still others, particularly beginners, receive only the first few words of a prophetic message, accompanied by a strong sense that the Lord wants them to begin speaking, even before they know what they are going to say.

Those who prophesy at prayer meetings often say that they prophesy in response to a certain inner urge or "anointing," which they believe to be from God.

Sometimes, but not always, this impulse is accompanied by physical sensations — "butterflies" in the stomach, tightness in the chest, warmth, tingling sensations, or other signs. Leaders in the movement acknowledge that such feelings may or may not accompany a genuine call to speak a prophetic message, adding that such sensations are not reliable indicators of whether the urge is from God.

"Often," says Yocum, "more than one person will receive the same prophecy. On many occasions I have heard people prophesy a message exactly as I heard it from the Lord myself — word for word the same. Occurrences like that can build up our confidence in the prophetic gift."[4]

Charismatic prophecy consists of two parts — hearing the word of God and speaking it. Merely hearing a message from God does not constitute prophecy and neither does the speaking of it unless God directs the person to speak. Sometimes, prophetic messages are delivered at prayer meetings as an "interpretation" of an utterance that was spoken in tongues. In such instances, one person may speak in tongues and the unintelligible utterance be followed by an interpretation, often given by a member who has a recognized prophetic gift.

The prophecies most frequently heard at prayer meetings are messages of encouragement: "Do not be afraid, I, your God, am with you always." "My children, stand firm in my love which no evil can withstand." Such messages are simple, but they accurately reflect God's tender concern for us. Spoken in the first person, they convey the immediacy of a message directly to us from him.

Messages of admonition are sometimes spoken in prophecy, too. In these, the tone is that of a concerned father, rather than a critical adversary. It may be spoken in the first person or the speaker may simply relate something he or she believes God is trying to tell the group.

A prophetic message of this type might urge members of a prayer group to stop gossiping about one another or remind them that they have allowed other concerns to become more important than their relationship with God.

Yocum, in his book *Prophecy*, tells how such a message helped a young married couple when they first began coming to The Word of God prayer meetings: "They were seeking God, but were not convinced that He could be found in Christianity. They were also being troubled by jealousy and animosity in their own relationship. During one of the first meetings they attended, the husband was feeling great doubt that Christianity held out any hope for him at all. He silently offered an almost despairing prayer, asking for some sign that God could be found among Christians. At the very moment he concluded that prayer, another young man stood to speak: 'I believe that God has shown me a young married couple present at this meeting tonight' (there were about six hundred people at the meeting). 'These people are seeking God, but are encountering doubt and confusion. Furthermore, they are having difficulty in their own relationship because of anger and

jealousy.' He went on to tell them, in the name of the
Lord, that if they forgave one another and trusted in God,
God would reveal himself to them and strengthen their
marriage. Of course, the young husband was
thunderstruck. This person had perfectly described their
situation, and offered a solution at the very moment he
had asked for it. The young man who spoke to them in
prophecy had neither met them nor ever heard of them.
That young couple heeded God's word, repented of their
anger with one another, and are now living happily as
Christians."

That incident recalls Saint Paul's observation that
"if an unbeliever or an uninitiate enters while all are
uttering prophecy, he will be taken to task by all and
called to account by all, and the secret of his heart will be
laid bare. Falling prostrate, he will worship God, crying
out, 'God is truly among you' " (1 Corinthians 14:24-25).

Many charismatics tell of other incidents in which
God used prophecy to guide them or their prayer groups
in decision making. Yocum cites at least two instances in
which a group he was working with received clear,
practical, and beneficial direction in prophecy. In one
case, he says, the Lord told the group, "Put your own
relationships in order first." In the other, the Lord gave
specific guidance to individuals to help them accomplish
a set of goals.

This kind of prophetic guidance is, perhaps, the most
controversial aspect of charismatic prophecy in the
modern church. It involves two dangers: the first is that
Christians will rely so heavily on supernatural guidance
that they expect God to make their decisions for them. I

once knew a person who prayed regularly and insisted that the Lord directed all her decisions. Her method was to pray and wait for some sort of spiritual nudge in the right direction. Whenever she was asked if she would help in some church or neighborhood project, her answer was always the same: "I'll pray about it." Later, she would say, "I prayed, but I didn't hear the Lord calling me to do that." It's good to receive spiritual nudges in prayer, but often the Lord asks for our help through the voices of those who need our help.

The other danger in relying on prophecy is failing to distinguish between an authentic word from the Lord and a message that comes from another source. Modern Christians have to ask, as first-century Christians did, "How do we know that this prophecy is actually a revelation of God's will?"

How do we know that it is not merely a manifestation of human imagination, or even a deliberate attempt by a self-styled prophet to manipulate others? How do we know that the prophecy doesn't stem from some darker source: a spirit of pride, of anger, or of jealousy? If we expect the Holy Spirit to speak to us, we should be aware that unholy spirits will also seek to distract us and confuse us in our quest for God's truth.

The problem of discerning true and false prophecy has been with the church from the beginning. Discerning the truth and authenticity of prophecy is always risky. Hearing the word of God depends on faith as well as judgment, and prophecies never come with a written guarantee, signed by Jesus, declaring that a prophet and his words accurately represent the mind of the Lord.

"The only credentials a prophet has is the word of God," Father Francis Martin, an internationally known charismatic leader, once told a group of Catholic charismatic priests. It is up to those who listen to the prophet to determine whether or not the message is authentic.[5]

One of the major reasons why Christian prophecy has not flourished in most centuries is probably the recognition of this problem. Since the time of Montanus, the church has been understandably wary of prophecy or, for that matter, any kind of personal revelation experienced by members of the church.

For most of the church's history, the judging of prophecy has seldom been an urgent matter because in most ages the prophetic gift wasn't widely exercised. But today, with millions of Catholics involved in a worldwide prophetic movement, the need is obvious. Fortunately, leaders in the Catholic charismatic renewal are well aware of the need to test the truth and authenticity of prophecy.

"I don't believe that we can come to an absolute determination that any particular prophecy today is genuine," Yocum admits. At the same time, Yocum and other charismatics recognize certain principles that prayer groups can and should use to judge whether or not a prophecy is from God. The principles involve the testing of the message itself, the spirit of the message, and its effect on the people to whom it was delivered.

The message itself, if it is from God, cannot contradict Scripture or the authentic teaching of the church. Obviously, if someone prophesies a message contrary to the teachings of Christ, it is not from God. Some Catholic charismatics even declare that authentic prophecy cannot contradict the authority of those in leadership of a prayer group. Father Michael Scanlan, president of The Franciscan University of Steubenville and chairman of the editorial board of the charismatic magazine *New Covenant*, says prophecy "must be consistent with God's word in scripture, the teaching office of the church, and established pastoral authority."

But just because a message agrees with Scripture doesn't make it an authentic prophecy. Authentic prophecy is spoken in response to God's urging through the Holy Spirit. So one of the ways charismatics test prophecy is to look for evidence that the prophecy was inspired by God. Charismatics declare that those who have received the Holy Spirit and who seek a close relationship with the Lord become increasingly able to recognize his voice. Some people seem to be more able than others in this regard. One of the charismatic gifts enumerated by Saint Paul is the "ability to distinguish between spirits" (1 Corinthians 12:10).

Yocum declares that the first test of whether something comes from the Holy Spirit is "the response in our own heart and spirit." The second is whether the prophetic message has a loving spiritual tone and effect. The Lord may sometimes speak a stern message, but he doesn't condemn. The third test, says Yocum, is whether the utterance glorifies Jesus. A more revealing indicator of a prophecy's authenticity is its effect on those who hear it. Does it cause division in the prayer meeting or does it bring new life to the group? One of the major purposes of the charismatic gifts is the building-up of the body of Christ, and Christians should expect that if God speaks through prophecy he will strengthen them in love.

In addition, prayer groups generally weigh not only the prophecy but also the maturity and wisdom of those who prophesy. Any person baptized into the life of Jesus Christ may hear the Lord's voice in some of the ways described above and may occasionally be called by the Lord to share God's message with others. But before such a person is recognized as a prophet, those abilities should be demonstrated over a period of months or years. When such a person speaks, a prayer community can be more confident that the message is from God than if it were spoken by a person whose prophetic gifts were not known.

Yocum believes that the personal life of the prophet is also an important consideration. "I would go so far as to say that even if an individual who is living immorally gets a genuine word from the Lord from time to time, we ought in principle to be very wary of accepting something from that individual. If God wants to speak to us, He can find individuals who are more reliable in themselves."[6]

Father Martin declares that as a person grows in prophetic ministry, that person attains more credibility as a prophet. "The greatest example," says Father Martin, "is Jesus. Jesus said, 'The Father loves you; the Father sent me to have the kingdom break in on you; to take upon myself all those things that weigh you down and to break bondage in this world and in the underworld.' Everyone said, 'Wow, that's terrific, Jesus.' And then he grew into his prophecy and died in an

act of love and that's what makes his prophecy ring
true." According to Father Martin, everything Jesus
said took on new life at the resurrection: "Even his
words rose again."[7]

Jesus, of course, is *the* revelation on which the
Catholic faith is built, and all prophecy must be rejected
if it denies Christ's teaching or the meaning of his life,
death, and resurrection as taught by the church he
founded.

Catholics and Pentecostals sometimes describe the
manifestation of charismatic gifts as a return to the
power and zeal that existed in the church of the first
century, but one important difference between the first
and twentieth centuries must be taken into account. The
church of the first century relied much more heavily on
the oral tradition: the teaching and preaching of the
apostles. The writings that now make up the New
Testament were still being written and, at that time,
were not yet recognized by the church as canonical.
Some of the Christian manuscripts of the first century,
like Paul's letters, became part of the New Testament,
but many others did not.

The teachings of Christ were transmitted and
interpreted by the apostles, usually by word of mouth.
There is no clear proof that there were any major
Christian writings prior to A.D. 50. During the first few
centuries, the church gradually recognized certain
writings of the apostles to be uniquely inspired. Those
writings became the New Testament.

In the first-century church, prophecy could not be
judged in the light of New Testament writings because

the canon of the New Testament had not yet been defined. It was judged in the light of the oral traditions of the apostles. Today, prophecy must be judged according to both Holy Scripture and Holy Tradition.

It is a positive sign that leaders within the Catholic charismatic renewal seem to be unanimous in recognizing that prophecy can never speak with as much authority as Scripture or the teaching authority of the church.

CHAPTER NINE

Visions and Apparitions

Visions and apparitions, like prophecy, are a form of revelation, a means by which God reveals his word. The Roman Catholic Church makes a distinction between "public revelation" — given to the church through Jesus and the apostles — and "private revelation," in which God continues to speak to individuals or groups of individuals.

When the church speaks of public revelation, it refers to the birth of Jesus, his life, death, and resurrection, and his teachings, imparted to the church through the traditions of the apostles and recorded in Holy Scripture. It is upon this public revelation that our creed and the basic beliefs of our faith are founded.

The church teaches that public revelation ended with the death of the last apostle. That does not mean that all revelation ceased when the last apostle died, but it does mean that any new revelation must be judged by whether it is consistent with the revelation given to the church some twenty centuries ago. Prophetic visions, apparitions, and charismatic prophecy all fall within the realm of private revelation. That means that however authentic they may be, they can never have as much authority as Holy Scripture or Sacred Tradition.

Private revelation is usually, but not always, directed toward a single individual or a small group of individuals. Many, if not most, Catholics have had experiences in which they felt convinced that God was, in some manner, trying to speak to them in order to encourage them, to help them live more positively, to guide them, or simply to reassure them of his love.

Such messages don't ordinarily come to us in a voice that we can hear with our ears. More often, they are words that arise in our hearts and our minds.

The church recognizes that God speaks in this manner to many persons, whether they are Catholics, Protestants, Jews, Buddhists, or even people who profess no religion at all. In fact, many nonbelievers have become Christians after hearing God calling to them in some such manner.

Similarly, such messages sometimes come to us in a visual manner — usually as images that form in our minds, and sometimes as images that are actually perceived with the eyes.

Private revelation of this sort is most often given for the benefit of an individual, but not always. Often in its two-thousand-year history, the church has been influenced and guided (and occasionally misguided) through private revelations. Some of these influential private revelations are well-known.

The Roman emperor Constantine, although he was not yet a Christian, once had a vision that led to an important turning point in the history of the church. Preparing to meet his enemy Maxentius in battle near Rome in 312, Constantine prayed to his god, Apollo, asking for a sign of victory in the coming battle. Instead, he saw a vision of a flaming cross and, beneath it, the words *In hoc signo vinces* ("Under this sign you will conquer"). The experience eventually led to Constantine's conversion, but even before that, it led him to abandon the empire's persecution of Christians.

Saint Francis of Assisi's remarkable impact on the church stemmed, in part, from visions and dreams that guided his actions and, as we have already seen, the revelations experienced by Saint Catherine of Siena had an influence on the actions of popes.

The visions of Blessed Juliana of Cornillon in the thirteenth century led to the establishment of the feast of Corpus Christi and those of Margaret Mary Alacoque in the seventeenth century led to the establishment in the Catholic Church of devotion to the Sacred Heart of Jesus.

For at least seventeen hundred years, a certain type of private revelation, involving apparitions of the Virgin

Mary, has occurred from time to time among some of the faithful. Gregory the Thaumaturge reported seeing Mary in the third century and so did Saint Athanasius in the fourth.

The church credits thousands of conversions among the Indians of Central America to Mary's appearance in 1531 to an Indian named Juan Diego. Juan Diego's *tilma*, or cloak, was miraculously marked with an image of the lady who had appeared to him on a hillside near what would later become the center of Mexico City. It has been estimated that in the decade that followed, some eight million Indians were baptized. The image and the cloak have remained remarkably intact for more than four and a half centuries and are now housed at the Basilica of Our Lady of Guadalupe in Mexico City near the site of the apparitions.

During the last century and a half, dozens of other Marian apparitions have been reported. Of these, most have been rejected by the church, but a few have been declared by the church to be worthy of belief.

Among the better known are the Marian apparitions that have occurred in France (at La Salette in 1846 and at Lourdes in 1858); at Knock, Ireland, in 1879; and at Fátima, Portugal, in 1917. Other apparitions approved by the church occurred in Paris (1830), Pontmain, France (1871), Beuraing, Belgium (1932-1933), and Banneaux, Belgium (1933). Several of these apparitions have involved prophetic messages attributed to our Lady.

La Salette is a village in the diocese of Grenoble in southeastern France. On September 19, 1846, while Melanie Mathieu-Calvat, fifteen, and Maximin Giraud, eleven, were herding cows on a mountain above the village, they saw in a glen what they later described as a beautiful lady in a globe of light, splendidly attired but weeping. The children were afraid at first, but the figure beckoned them nearer and gave the children a message that she said they were to tell "all her people": that unless they repented of religious apathy she would be forced to "let fall the arm of her Son." The lady also entrusted to each of the children a secret which the other could not hear.

The children repeated the message they had received, but most of the villagers at first dismissed their story. These were not pious children. They and their families, like many other Catholic families in the region, had become lax about prayer and reception of the sacraments. Maximin had a reputation as a mischievous boy.

But the children, when examined separately, agreed with each other in every detail of the apparition and both of them clung to their story in spite of bribes and threats. As news of the apparition spread, a great conversion swept the area. At the site of the apparition, a previously dried-up spring began to flow and many miraculous cures were reported.

After a five-year investigation, Bishop Philibert de Bruillard of Grenoble declared the apparition had the characteristics of truth, thereby authorizing the faithful to practice devotion to Our Lady of La Salette.

Provincial France was also the setting for a series of Marian apparitions that led to establishment of the best-known healing shrine in the history of the church. It was in the small village of Lourdes, at the foot of the Pyrenees in southwestern France, that the Virgin Mary first appeared in 1858 to Bernadette Soubirous, the fourteen-year-old daughter of a poverty-stricken miller.

The apparitions began at a grotto near the Gave River on February 11. The first time it happened, the girl was attracted to a glowing light in the grotto. As she looked, she recognized the form of a woman dressed in white and wearing a blue sash. The girl knelt and prayed her rosary, but when the smiling lady beckoned her to come closer, Bernadette was timid and did not move. The lady vanished.

Over the next five months, over the objections of her parents, Bernadette continued to go to the grotto, where she saw the lady eighteen times. During the first apparitions, the lady remained silent but smiled at Bernadette.

On February 18, the woman spoke to Bernadette for the first time, asking Bernadette to continue coming to the grotto for fifteen days. "I do not promise to make you happy in this world but in the next," she said. Villagers who had accompanied Bernadette to the grotto saw and heard nothing. A few days later, the lady delivered a message. The lady said she desired "penitence," not just from Bernadette but from all. "Pray to God for the conversion of sinners," she told the girl.

On one occasion, the lady told Bernadette to drink and wash herself at a fountain. Seeking to obey, the child dug at the floor of the grotto but found nothing except mud. Nevertheless, she put it to her lips as if to drink. A crowd of spectators saw only a fourteen-year-old girl smearing her face with mud as if she were deranged.

After that incident the local police commissioner told Bernadette she must not go again to the grotto; but the next day, in obedience to the lady, she went anyway. She found more than six hundred people waiting for her, standing at the edge of a small pool of water that had bubbled up through the mud. Eventually, the flow from the spring was to reach as much as thirty-two thousand gallons a day and sick people who applied its waters to their bodies began to report miraculous cures.

On March 2, the lady asked Bernadette to tell the local priests that a chapel should be built at the grotto and that people should come there in procession. Abbé Peramale, dean of the district, personally believed that the apparitions were authentic appearances of the Virgin Mary, but he knew, too, that there was no official recognition that this was so. At that point, the church was obliged to assume that they were nothing more than flights of Bernadette's imagination. To help resolve his dilemma, the abbé made Bernadette promise to ask the lady to identify herself.

On March 25, the lady told Bernadette, "I am the Immaculate Conception." Bernadette apparently had no idea what the words meant, but Abbé Peramale did. The dogma of the Immaculate Conception, declaring that Mary had been "preserved from every taint of original sin" from the moment of her conception, had been proclaimed by Pope Pius IX only four years earlier, in 1854.

Bernadette, who later entered the Sisters of Nevers, died in 1879 and was canonized on the feast of the

Immaculate Conception in 1933. In 1862, less than four
years after the apparitions began, the bishop of Tarbes
released a letter commending Lourdes as a site for
Marian devotions. Four chapels now stand near the site
of the apparitions.

More than five thousand cures have been attributed
to the intercession of Our Lady of Lourdes. When visitors
to Lourdes report cures, they are first examined there by
a medical bureau of physicians. Persons whose cases
appear to be valid are asked to return a year later for
confirmation. Approved cases are forwarded to a
commission in the diocese of the person cured. The
bishop of that see then makes a pronouncement on the
nature of the cure. To date, sixty-four of the cures at
Lourdes have been categorized by the church as
"miraculous."

In the apparitions at Lourdes and at La Salette, Mary
spoke in a conversational manner to those who saw her,
but there have been other apparitions in which she spoke
in a more prophetic tone. Perhaps the most notable
example was a series of apparitions seen by three
shepherd children in the parish of Fátima, in central
Portugal, in 1917.

At the time, the First World War was raging and
Russia was on the verge of revolution. The world was
rapidly moving away from the Christian faith and putting
increasing hope for the future in social philosophies that
rejected or ignored the primacy of God.

The Fátima apparitions began on May 13, 1917,
during World War I, in which Portugal was fighting
against Germany. On that day, Lucia dos Santos, ten, and

her cousins, Francisco Marto, nine, and his sister, Jacinta, seven, were playing as they tended sheep in a natural depression on a hillside, known locally as the Cova da Iria. Suddenly there was a brilliant light that the children, at first, mistook for a flash of lightning. As they sought shelter, they saw what they described as a large ball of light near the top of a small tree. Inside the ball, they could see the glowing form of a beautiful woman. The children were frightened until the woman spoke to them in a comforting manner, telling them not to fear. The two girls could both see and hear her. Francisco said he was able to see but not hear her.

She asked them to return on the thirteenth day of every month for six months and promised that at the end of that time she would reveal her identity and her purpose. She left them after urging them to "say the rosary to obtain peace for the world, and the end of the war."

Lucia's parents scoffed at the story the children told and her mother scolded Lucia for lying. But, in obedience to the lady, the children prayed their rosaries. On June 13, a small crowd accompanied them to the Cova. Again the lady appeared, but only the three children could see her. On this occasion she told Lucia that she would soon take Francisco and Jacinta to heaven but that Lucia would remain on earth to help establish devotion to the Immaculate Heart of Mary.

The third apparition, on July 13, included a number of prophecies. After showing the children a vision of hell, the lady declared that unless people stopped offending God there would be another war, even more terrible than the present one. She went on to declare that she had come to ask the consecration of Russia to her Immaculate Heart and to urge people to participate in a "Communion of reparation" on first Saturdays. "If they listen to my requests, Russia will be converted and there will be peace," she said. "If not, she will scatter her errors through the world, provoking wars and persecution of the church." Some of the persecutions would affect the pope, she said. But she also prophesied that Russia would be converted, bringing a period of peace to the world.

Clearly, those words of Mary were not intended only for the three children but for all of suffering humanity. But there were other messages, too, given to the children with instructions that they were not to share them with others.

After that, the crowds of spectators increased dramatically, but political radicals and anticlericals ridiculed the events. The Portuguese government at that time was openly hostile to religion, and some civic officials felt that the events at Fátima should be halted. That opinion was shared by the civil prefect of Ourem who personally prevented the children from returning to the Cova on August 13. He took them into custody and had them held for two days while officials tried unsuccessfully to frighten the children into revealing the secrets entrusted to them.

On October 13, a crowd estimated at fifty thousand to seventy thousand waited at the Cova. The lady appeared to the children and again called for repentance and prayers for peace. She asked that a chapel be built on the site, to honor her as "Our Lady of the Rosary." She promised that the war would end soon — on that very day or soon after, according to Lucia.

Then the lady vanished. All three children then saw visions in the sky of the Holy Family. Until that point, the day had been dark and wet, but as the apparition ended, the sun appeared. Many in the crowd said they watched the sun tremble, rotate, and dance above the heads of the people. A journalist who that morning had publicly ridiculed the apparitions was no longer scoffing when he wrote about the events in the Lisbon daily *O Seculo* two days later.

After the events of October 13, the apparitions received widespread public acceptance, although the church had not yet expressed an official opinion on their credibility. The war did not end quickly as Lucia had said it would and there were a number of discrepancies between the accounts given by Lucia and those given by reliable witnesses. These were taken into account during a canonical process of inquiry that began in 1922 and lasted for seven years. Finally, in 1930, the bishop of Leiria declared that the apparitions were worthy of credence and authorized devotion to Our Lady of Fátima.

Francisco died in 1919 and Jacinta in 1920. Lucia became a Dorothean lay sister and later wrote about the apparitions, giving further details about them. Lucia also wrote that in 1915 (some say 1916), she had seen apparitions of an angel. However, the later writings were not submitted to the same canonical processes that the original reports underwent.

What is striking about the Marian apparitions at Fátima is the prophetic role of Mary, calling her children to a renewal of faith and of prayer in the midst of war and violence. This is an important message for our time. Our century has seen almost continuous war — including two world wars, two cities destroyed with nuclear weapons, and genocide against the Armenians by the Turks, Europe's Jews by the Germans, and the people of Cambodia (now Kampuchea) by a fanatic Communist clique led by some of their own countrymen. Our Lady, at Fátima, is trying to lead us back to her Son and his way of peace.

The theme of peace begun at Fátima has been repeated in apparitions seen by several young people in Medjugorje, in the diocese of Mostar, Yugoslavia. It must be pointed out that the church has not yet made any declaration as to the believability of the Medjugorje apparitions and they have created some controversy among Yugoslavian church officials who are divided over their authenticity.

At any rate, the Medjugorje apparitions are strongly prophetic in nature and they have continued far longer than the other Marian apparitions we have discussed. I first visited Medjugorje with my wife, Anne, in January, 1984. The following account was given to us verbally by priests and religious at Saint James Church in Medjugorje. Therefore, some details may differ from other accounts.

The apparitions began shortly after six o'clock on the evening of June 24, 1981, when five teenagers from Bijakovici, one of Medjugorje's five villages, were walking on the slopes of Podbrdo, one of the rocky, semi-arid hills that surround the valley of Medjugorje. As the young people were walking, they were surprised to see a great light about six hundred fifty feet ahead of them.

As they watched, the light began to take the form of a human figure. The sight lasted only a few minutes, after which the surprised youths returned to their village at the foot of the hill and began telling other people what they had seen. The next evening, the children went back up the hill, accompanied by curious villagers, both young and old; among them was Jakov Colo, who was ten years old.

The figure appeared again, standing above them on the steep, rocky slope and beckoning the children to come closer. They raced easily up the hill, although it is covered with boulders and thornbushes. Later, the children would say that they had felt as if they were being swept along by a supernatural power. Some of the children had brought holy water and sprinkled it in the direction of the figure, declaring, "If you are Satan, be gone!"

The figure, which appeared as a woman standing upon a cloud, smiled and said, "I am the Mother of God." This time the apparition was seen and heard by little Jakov as well as the five who had seen it the first time.

The six children, including Jakov, continued to visit the hillside regularly and saw the lady on each occasion. By the third day of the alleged apparitions, several thousand spectators were accompanying the young people to the hill. By the end of June, the crowds had grown to fifteen thousand.

On August 12, local authorities ordered both the children and the crowds to stay away from the hillside.

After that, the children gathered for prayers in the church and the apparitions continued there.

As a result, the curious spectators became churchgoers eager to do penance and receive the sacraments of the church.

Franciscan Father Tomislav Vlasic, the children's spiritual director who was assigned to the parish soon after the apparitions began, said he became convinced of their validity not long after he arrived.

"I was open to see what was going on," he said through a translator. "As a priest, I had to be." He said he had the children examined by doctors who found them to be healthy and normal.

Records have been kept of all the messages attributed to the Madonna by the children, but not all of these have been made public. Members of the Franciscan community at Medjugorje say it would be impossible to do this without giving a complete, chronological description of all the apparitions.

Ten of the messages were allegedly given to the children as "secrets," which they were instructed to divulge only to appropriate church authorities. One of these is reported to be a promise of "a permanent visible sign" at the place of the first apparition.

Members of the Franciscan community here have made public what they say are the more important and more interesting messages.

When Father Vlasic was asked if the messages have a common theme, he nodded and replied, "Mir" (Croatian for "peace").

In one of the messages, the Madonna is alleged to

have spoken to the visionaries about "tension among world powers" that is bringing humanity to "the brink of disaster." She is said to have told the children that prayer and fasting can stop even war.

Yet peace, according to the messages, is the responsibility of individual Christians who must seek it first in their own hearts through prayer and fasting, repentance, conversion, and faith.

Not surprisingly, prayer and fasting have become a way of life among the twenty-five hundred Catholics here. Virtually everyone in the parish fasts every Friday, many of them taking only bread and water. Many, particularly among the teenagers of the parish, are reportedly fasting two or even three days a week.

Other signs of church renewal in Medjugorje are increased Mass attendance, widespread participation in charismatic prayer groups, frequent reception of the sacrament of reconciliation, reports of many conversions and healings, and a particularly strong degree of religious commitment among young people.

As I write this the apparitions that began in 1981 have continued on an almost daily basis, although some of the original six children no longer see them.

When my wife and I visited Medjugorje, we went to the site where the first of the apparitions occurred and later we watched the young visionaries during an apparition in a room attached to the sacristy of Saint James Church. It was a fascinating experience but not very revealing. Simply watching someone else have a spiritual experience did nothing to verify or discredit the validity of what was happening.

But we did find in Medjugorje a positive sign of God's grace. We found a parish renewed in faith, piety, and love, whose members were openly living as devout Christians in a country whose government denies the existence of God.

Hundreds of thousands of pilgrims from throughout the world have visited Medjugorje. Most of the pilgrims have been Catholics, but there have also been Protestants, Orthodox, and even Muslim pilgrims. After returning from Medjugorje, I spoke to David DuPlessis, a well-known American Pentecostal leader who had visited Medjugorje in 1983. He, too, was impressed by the strong renewal of Christian faith he had seen there. "I cannot say if Mary is there," he told me, "but I can tell you that Jesus is."

Yet, as noted above, the apparitions at Medjugorje have not, at this point, been declared by the church to be worthy of belief — and the same is true of most alleged Marian apparitions. There have, in fact, been hundreds of purported apparitions about which the church has either remained silent or has declared to be unworthy of belief.

The church exercises great caution whenever it examines the credibility of apparitions. Ordinarily, it is the responsibility of the local bishop to examine the facts, to determine the trustworthiness of the witnesses, and to weigh the probability of fraud or error. The church must always begin with a presumption that the apparitions are suspect.

And even if the bishop publishes his official approval of such events, he does not guarantee their authenticity.

Rather, he declares merely that they do not appear to be false, that they do not contradict the doctrines of the church, and that the faithful have permission to believe them with caution.

The church must always presume, until shown otherwise, that alleged apparitions of Mary are *not* authentic, according to an American bishop with experience in that field.

"God doesn't usually intervene in such ways, so the burden of proof is on the other side," Bishop Anthony J. Bevilacqua of Pittsburgh told me. "You always presume that it's not authentic."

The responsibility for determining whether a claimed apparition is authentic rests with the church, said Bishop Bevilacqua, who once investigated such a claim.

"The church is the only discerner of the authenticity of such events," he said. Within the church, he added, such discernment rests with the hierarchy.

Bishop Bevilacqua's experience stems from an investigation he undertook on behalf of the diocese of Brooklyn several years ago when he examined claims that an alleged visionary named Veronica Lueken was seeing apparitions and receiving messages from Mary in New York. Bishop Bevilacqua, who investigated those claims while serving in the Brooklyn diocese, said that in spite of wide popular acceptance, the alleged Bayside apparitions did not meet the tests required by the church.

In investigating such claims, the church looks carefully into three separate areas.

First, it interviews the alleged visionary or

visionaries to determine if their reports are credible and consistent.

Second, it examines the content of any alleged messages to determine if these are consistent with the teachings of Christ as passed on by his church.

Third, it seeks evidence of supernatural intervention. "Usually," said Bishop Bevilacqua, "that means some kind of miraculous sign."

Why is the church, which seeks to promote faith in an unseen God, so hard to convince when it comes to apparitions?

Because, explained Bishop Bevilacqua, it cannot endorse any teaching or alleged revelation that would add to or detract from the truth revealed by Jesus Christ.

As Bishop Bevilacqua points out, the beliefs and teaching of the church are founded upon a revelation that was given to the world by God nearly two thousand years ago. That revelation cannot change and any private revelation that does not conform to the public revelation of Jesus and his apostles cannot be accepted by the church as authentic.

●

CHAPTER TEN

●

Is God Trying to Tell Us Something?

●

God isn't far away from us. He is much closer than our minds are able to imagine. Jesus told his disciples "that all may be one / as you, Father, are in me, and I in you" (John 17:21). As followers of Jesus, we are invited into an intimate relationship with God.

This mysterious relationship between ourselves and God is impossible for us to fully comprehend with our minds, but it is more than an abstract concept. It is a real relationship. And as in any relationship between persons who love each other, there is a need for communication so that the relationship can thrive and grow. Communication builds relationships. Just as communication between husbands and wives builds strong marriages, communication between God and us builds a strong church.

We communicate with God through prayer. Many of us tend to think of prayer as an exercise in which we do the talking and God does the listening, but that is one-sided prayer. We also need to take the time to be silent and listen to what God is saying to us. God is a speaker as well as a listener and he communicates with us far more faithfully than we communicate with him. In fact, God is constantly trying to get our attention, but we have an unfortunate tendency to ignore him.

Many Catholics, particularly priests and religious, remind themselves every day of the need to listen to the Lord. Morning prayer in the Divine Office, recited daily as the worldwide prayer of the church, contains these lines of exhortation: "For he is our God, / and we are the people he shepherds, / the flock he guides. / Oh, that today you would hear his voice: / 'Harden not your hearts. . .' " (Psalm 95:7-8).

Unless we want to close ourselves off from the intimate relationship that God wants with us, we need to soften our hearts and hear his voice. All of us tend to cling to our own thoughts, ideas, and prejudices, but as long as we do that, we will never hear God. We need to let go of our own preconceived ideas and allow God to speak to us.

Not all of us are called to be prophets, at least not in the sense of delivering God's word to others, but each of us can learn to hear his voice. All Christians are called to a relationship with God, and the more we enter into that relationship the more we can expect to hear God's word. The Lord may speak to us through Scripture, through our pastors, through the inspired teaching and preaching of others within the church, or through the cries of those who have been denied justice or a rightful share of the world's goods.

God may also speak to us in our own hearts. Many people, perhaps all, have had experiences in which words, ideas, or thoughts seem to form unexpectedly somewhere within themselves. For some people, these seem almost to have been spoken by a voice. For others, there is no voice; rather, it is a message in words that are thought or felt rather than spoken. Sometimes the experience doesn't involve words at all but mental images — visions or pictures that convey an idea. Sometimes the experience is simply a conviction that arises, that seems to come from a source other than our own knowledge or wisdom. Certainly, there is ample evidence in the Old and New Testaments as well as in the lives of the saints, martyrs, and mystics of the church to show that God sometimes communicates with people in this manner.

The Catholic theologian Karl Rahner declares that "to deny the fundamental possibility of private revelation one would have to be prepared to maintain that all revelation is impossible — which would be equivalent to a denial of Christianity — or that no revelation is conceivable except in a community and for a community."

Because of the growth of the charismatic renewal,

private revelations and other charismatic gifts are much
more widely accepted among Catholics now than they
were a decade ago. But even before the first public
stirrings of the charismatic renewal, many theologians
recognized private revelation as a sign of God's
presence. The *New Catholic Encyclopedia* declared in
1967 that "charismatic graces such as private
revelations are a normal manifestation of the presence
of the Spirit of Christ in the Mystical Body and of His
continued guidance of the Church."

A word of caution is necessary here. God may indeed
speak to individuals today, but such "private
revelation," even though it may be authentic, cannot add
to or subtract from the public revelation of the Christ
event.

The Christ event was a special kind of revelation,
given for the entire church. It defines for every Catholic
believer the basic truths of our faith. The church teaches
that public revelation was closed with the death of the
last apostle, thereby acknowledging the life, death, and
resurrection of Christ as the supreme revelation of all
time.

But just because the church has already received its
central revelation in the person of Christ does not mean
that God has now become distant. On the contrary,
through the workings of the Holy Spirit, that same Jesus
who *is* the central revelation of our church continues to
speak to and through his people in private revelation,
including prophecy.

Thomas Aquinas declared in his *Summa
Theologica* that it is not the purpose of prophecy to

develop new doctrines of faith but, rather, to direct
human activity. In other words, while prophecy cannot
add to or subtract from the essential truths of our faith, it
can nevertheless remind us of those truths. It can call us
to be more faithful to those truths and to trust and obey
God. True prophecy consistently urges Christians to
recognize the lordship of Jesus and to recognize and
serve him in the needy of the world.

The church does not require Catholics to believe
those things that are expressed only in private
revelation. In fact, Catholics are permitted to believe
things expressed in this manner only if they do not
contradict Scripture or the authoritative teachings of the
church. In some cases, the church or individual pastors
may encourage certain devotions based on private
revelation, but Catholics are not obliged to practice
them.

Some revelations may be restricted to particular
groups, to particular times. Most of the prophecies
spoken in charismatic circles are words of
encouragement or direction that clearly apply only to the
life of that particular group at a particular time of its
development.

It is not uncommon, within charismatic communities
and prayer groups, to hear prophecies addressed to
specific situations.

Bruce Yocum, the well-known charismatic author
mentioned earlier in Chapter 8, declares, "Prophecy
never extends the doctrinal revelation of Scripture. But
sometimes it is more than applying scriptural revelation
to particular circumstances. Prophecy may reveal God's

mind about particular situations in a way that Scripture does not.''

Hearing God's word in prophecy can be an inspiring experience that produces abundant good among a body of believers. But there is an undeniable danger. Those who speak prophecy are human beings and, like all human beings, are capable of error. In some cases, they may also be capable of deception or even outright fraud. It is therefore necessary to carefully weigh and to judge prophecy or, in the words of Saint Paul, to ''test the spirits'' that inspire prophetic utterances.

The immediate responsibility for judging and testing prophecy rests with the leaders of the prayer group or community, but, ultimately, the responsibility rests on the teaching authority of the church. Catholics who belong to charismatic prayer groups should weigh all prophecy in the light of the teaching of their church. If it should happen that a prophecy denies the authentic teaching of the church, it is the responsibility of the prayer group leaders to point out the error. If a prayer group does not have leaders who are mature and gifted in discerning true prophecy from false, its members should refrain from exercising that gift.

But where mature leadership exists, prophecy can be an important gift to a community. It will be a great loss to the church if the gift of prophecy is seen only as an activity exercised among members of the charismatic renewal. I believe the day must come when the gift of prophecy and other gifts of the Holy Spirit will once again be recognized and used throughout the entire church. I suspect that each parish has potential prophets, teachers, and healers whose gifts need to be discovered and offered for the building-up of the parish just as charismatics use them for the building-up of their prayer communities.

In a sense, each of us is called to be a prophet. That is so because through our baptism we have entered into a personal relationship with God and have received the Holy Spirit. To the extent that we allow him to, the Spirit will draw us deeper and deeper into an intimate relationship with God.

A prophet is a person who has accepted this relationship and has learned to hear and recognize the word of God. God can speak through anyone, but a true prophet is someone who is awed by God's greatness but nevertheless dares to draw close to him. Like Moses, a true prophet enters into dialogue with God. It is through more or less constant dialogue that the prophet learns to hear and recognize God's word.

Becoming a prophet doesn't mean becoming perfect. It does mean loving God well enough to become familiar with his voice. All of us are sinners, but that doesn't mean we can't be prophets. Father Francis Martin tells us, "The Lord works with weak and sinful people because that's the only kind there is. He asks us to love one another, to risk for one another, to love Him enough to be with Him, to wait for Him, to treasure His word — and He promises us with all the power and strength and infinite might and love and commitment to us that is God: I will never leave you, I love you, I will strengthen you. I will never tell you anything that isn't true. But you can rely on me.''

The charismatics have done the church a great service by reawakening Catholics to the gifts of the Holy Spirit. At the same time, charismatics sometimes have a narrow view of what prophecy is. When charismatics speak of prophecy, they usually mean a gift that is exercised at prayer meetings or charismatic conferences in which God speaks in the first person through one of the prophets in the assembly.

But there are other prophetic voices in the church as well. The person who hears the word of God and proclaims it in a dynamic and relevant way is a prophet. It does not matter whether such an individual has heard God's voice in his or her heart, in Scripture, or in the cries of the oppressed. What does matter is that the person is attuned to the word of God and able to hear it.

Like Pope John Paul II, some of today's prophets hold positions of authority in the church. A pope or a bishop is not a prophet just because he wields authority but because he is able to hear and transmit God's word. There are and have been many prophetic voices in our century among those who serve the poor — men and women like Mother Teresa and the late Archbishop Oscar Romero of San Salvador. Not all of them are Catholics. Who can listen to the taped sermons and speeches of Martin Luther King, Jr., and fail to recognize the prophetic nature of his words?

Not everyone, of course, agrees on who today's prophets are. Many controversial figures in today's church are regarded as scoundrels by some and as prophets by others. Archbishop Marcel Lefebvre, Archbishop Raymond Hunthausen, Father Daniel

Berrigan, and anyone else whose ideas are widely
admired or detested is likely to fall into this category.
But a person isn't a prophet because he or she is
universally admired. Historically, prophets have
preached messages that made many people
uncomfortable.

A true prophet cannot be judged on the basis of
whether we agree with his words, but whether he is
speaking, on God's behalf, a message that is timely and
consistent with the teaching of Christ and his church.

The words of a true prophet do not contradict Holy
Scripture, but not everyone who accurately quotes
Scripture is a prophet. When Jesus fasted for forty days
in the desert, the devil himself tempted him by quoting
Scripture. When a prophet quotes Scripture, the purpose
isn't to prove a point or to add credibility to human
arguments, but to reveal what God is saying in a
particular time and situation.

Prophecy, says theologian Karl Rahner, "helps to
make the message of Jesus new, relevant and actual in
each changing age. It does not matter whether the
representatives of this charismatic prophecy in the
Church — the authors of religious renewal, the critics of
the Church and the society of their day, the discoverers
of new tasks for the Church and the faithful — are called
prophets or are given other names. They are mostly
comprised under the title of 'saints.' If such men do not
merely reaffirm general principles and apply them to
new cases, but display in their message something
creative and incalculable, with the force of historic
turning-points, so that they are legitimate and effective

in the Church, we may say that the Church has had a 'major or minor' prophet."

If the church is to benefit from the gift of prophecy, Catholics must welcome it, listen to it, judge it, and, if it is authentic, obey it.

The final authority for judging the authenticity of prophecy rests with the hierarchy. Catholics believe that the pope and the bishops are the successors of the apostles and that they are ultimately responsible for what is proclaimed as authentic teaching. But each believer is challenged to some extent to be a judge of prophecy. When we hear someone like Mother Teresa declaring that many Americans have forgotten how to love, we do not have to consult the hierarchy or wait for a pastoral letter to assure us that she is speaking God's truth.

When my wife and I visited Medjugorje, we were told that the Blessed Virgin Mary had appeared there and was urging believers to pray and fast for peace — particularly on Fridays. We were quite aware that the church had not made a declaration about the authenticity of the apparitions reported there, but we had no reservations about praying and fasting because we were convinced that apparitions or no apparitions, it would please God.

Our conviction rested on the fact that fasting for peace is fully consistent with Scripture and with the teachings of the church. In fact, during the year before our trip to Medjugorje, the American bishops, in their 1983 pastoral letter *The Challenge of Peace: God's Promise and Our Response*, had committed themselves to fast and to abstain from meat on each Friday of the year "for the cause of peace" and had urged others to make the same commitment.

The consistent teaching of the church through its interpretation of Scripture and Holy Tradition is the most reliable guide we have for recognizing the voice of the Lord in prophecy. Throughout the history of the church, the final authority in such matters has rested with the bishops of the church, in union with the pope.

The hierarchy not only has the final say in what constitutes authentic prophecy, but the hierarchy, like the rest of the church, needs to be open to hearing the word of God and, if necessary, being corrected by it. The hierarchy would be failing in its obligation to God if it were to allow false doctrine to be promoted through the charisms, but it would also be failing if it suppressed or inhibited charismatic gifts by which God was seeking to address his church.

"It is of course for the hierarchy to give the final assessment and verdict on charisms," declares theologian Karl Rahner, "but the hierarchy must also be prepared to be corrected by the charismatic element and to be aware of the protest against rigid institutionalism which is inherent in all charisms. As a testimony to the Spirit, the charisms, beside and along with the sacraments, go to make up the many-sided life of the Church. Their absence or suppression casts a shadow on the title deed of the Church, leads to conformity and inhibits all dynamism."[1]

The fears or reservations that Catholics usually express about the charismatic renewal — or, for that matter, any prophetic voice in the church — usually stem from well-intentioned desires to safeguard authentic Catholic doctrine and practice. Such fears were much more pronounced in the late 1960s and early 1970s, when the Catholic charismatic renewal was new, than they are now.

In the 1980s, the charismatic renewal has become an established institution. There are thousands of charismatic prayer groups now and, with few exceptions, they adhere closely to traditional Catholic teaching. In my opinion, many charismatic prayer groups have become so guarded in their use of the prophetic gift that they are in danger of stifling it.

In their efforts to assure the rest of the church that they are faithful to the doctrines of the church, some prayer groups have carefully delineated which persons in the group shall be recognized as prophets. In some cases, these safeguards have been developed so tightly it would be difficult for the Lord to use prophecy to introduce a radical message of any kind.

The charismatics are correct in insisting that prophecy must be tested — but it seems to me that such testing must always be exercised with a willingness to hear God's word, even when it makes us uncomfortable. Prophecy must be expressed before it can be tested. The danger is that the prophets will be overcontrolled; that the word of God will become so sanitized and safeguarded that it won't be heard in its full power.

Father Francis Martin has said that whoever wants to be a prophet has to realize that "love is going to get so loose in our heart that we're not going to remember anymore who the good guys are.'' A prophet, it seems to me, is always someone who speaks out of love for God, without being overly concerned about who may or may not agree with the message. The prophet's role is to speak, not to worry about how the message will be received. It is the role of the pastors, and ultimately of the hierarchy, to discern whether the prophet speaks the truth. It is the role of the prophet to give those pastors something to test. If the prophet remains silent out of fear of saying ''the wrong thing,'' the prophetic gift is being stifled.

Sometimes I envision the church as a boat. In my vision, the bark of Peter has sails to catch the wind and a rudder to guide it on its course. A nice breeze is blowing, but until the sails are raised, the boat simply sits dead in the water. As long as the boat is just sitting there, the person at the helm can move the rudder back and forth, but this has no effect. You can't steer a boat unless it's moving.

As soon as the sails are raised, they catch the wind and the boat begins to move. And as soon as the boat begins to move, the rudder can be used to steer it.

The members of the church, with all their gifts and talents, are the sails. The pope and the bishops are the rudder, and the wind is the Holy Spirit. Without the sails, the boat can go nowhere. But when the members are using their gifts, they catch the wind of the Holy Spirit and the church begins to move.

As soon as the bark of Peter moves, dangers loom. There are dangerous rocks and reefs that could damage it, perhaps even sink it. But a steady hand at the tiller carefully steers the boat past the rocks and holds it steady on course until it reaches its destination.

My point is that the hierarchy is responsible for guiding the boat but cannot by itself make the boat go anywhere. The movement of the church depends on the willingness of its members to use its gifts. Those who use their gifts for the church must run the risk of being misunderstood and those who steer must run the risk of misunderstanding. But those in authority and those they guide must trust and depend on one another as members of the Body of Christ.

If God is trying to tell us something, we must listen to him and heed his voice. We are the first generation on earth that holds the power to destroy virtually every person on the planet that God has entrusted to us. That same God has shared with us the power to give and receive love, to heal and to prophesy. I believe that what we do with this power will depend, ultimately, on how well we listen to God and how well we share his word with one another.

CHAPTER NOTES

Chapter 2

1. The "Urim and Thummim," occasionally mentioned
   in the early books of the Old Testament, were
   apparently an oracular device by which the early Jews
   were permitted to seek a "yes" or "no" answer from
   God. The Catholic Scripture scholar Father John L.
   McKenzie declares in his *Dictionary of the Bible*
   that "Urim and Thummim were an extremely
   primitive device for ascertaining the will of the deity;
   indeed, their use can scarcely be distinguished from
   divination. With the growth of religious enlightenment
   in Israel it seems that it was perceived that such a
   device had no place in the cult of Yahweh."

Chapter 6

1. Saint Justin Martyr, *Dialogue with Trypho*, in *The
   Fathers of the Church* (Catholic University of
   America Press, 1948), Vol. 6, p. 278.

2. *Didache*, in *The Fathers of the Church* (Catholic University of America Press, 1948), Vol. 1, pp. 179-180.
3. Ignatius of Antioch, *Letter to the Philadelphians*, in *The Fathers of the Church* (Catholic University of America Press, 1948), Vol. 1, pp. 115-116.
4. *Shepherd of Hermas*, Mandate 11.1, in *The Fathers of the Church* (Catholic University of America Press, 1948), Vol. 1, p. 280.
5. *Didache*, in *The Fathers of the Church* (Catholic University of America Press, 1948), Vol. 1, p. 182.
6. Ibid., p. 181.
7. Ibid., p. 180.
8. Tertullian, *On the Soul*, Ch. 9:3-4, in *The Fathers of the Church* (Catholic University of America Press, 1950), Vol. 10, p. 197.

Chapter 7

1. Jorgensen, Johannes, *Saint Catherine of Siena*, translated by Ingeborg Lund (Longmans, Green and Co., 1938), p. 220.
2. Scudder, Vita, *Saint Catherine of Siena as Seen in Her Letters* (E.P. Dutton, 1926), pp. 126-128.
3. Drane, Augusta Theodosia, *The History of St. Catherine of Siena* (Burns and Oates, 1880), p. 133.
4. Jorgensen, op. cit., p. 146.
5. Spalatinus, quoted in Joseph Milner's *History of the Church of Christ* (T. Cadell, 1819), Vol. V.

Chapter 8

1. O'Connor, Edward D., *The Pentecostal Movement in the Catholic Church* (Ave Maria Press, 1971), pp. 166-171.

2. Yocum, Bruce, *Prophecy* (Servant Books, 1976), pp. 39-45.
3. Scanlan, Michael, "Speaking for God," in *New Covenant*, July-August, 1986, p. 25.
4. Yocum, op. cit., p. 77.
5. Father Francis Martin — address at 1977 national Catholic Charismatic Conference for Priests at University of Steubenville.
6. "God Is Speaking to His People" (interview with Bruce Yocum), in *Pastoral Renewal*, Vol. 10, No. 11, June, 1986, pp. 183-184.
7. Father Francis Martin — address at 1977 national Catholic Charismatic Conference for Priests at University of Steubenville.

Chapter 10

1. Rahner, Karl, *Sacramentum Mundi* (Herder and Herder, 1968), Vol. 1, p. 284.

BIBLIOGRAPHY

Aune, David E., *Prophecy in Early Christianity and the Ancient Mediterranean World*. Grand Rapids, Mich.: William B. Eerdmans Publishing Co., 1983.

Blenkinsopp, Joseph. *A History of Prophecy in Israel*. Philadelphia: Westminster Press, 1983.

Chaine, Joseph. *God's Heralds*. Tr. by B. McGrath. New York: J.F. Wagner, 1955.

Chase, Mary Ellen. *The Prophets for the Common Reader*. New York: W.W. Norton & Co., Inc., 1963.

Clements, R.E. *Prophecy and Covenant*, Naperville, Ill.: Alec R. Allenson Inc., 1965.

Didache (or *Teachings of the Apostles*) in *The Fathers of the Church*, Vol. 1. Washington, D.C.: Catholic University of America Press, 1947.

Fichter, Joseph H. *The Catholic Cult of the Paraclete*. New York: Sheed & Ward, Inc., 1975.

Ignatius of Antioch, Saint. *To the Philadelphians* in *The Fathers of the Church*, Vol. 1. Washington, D.C.: Catholic University of America Press, 1947.

Jorstand, Erling. *The Holy Spirit in Today's Church.* Nashville, Tenn.: Abingdon Press, 1973.

Justin Martyr, Saint. *Dialogue with Trypho* in *The Fathers of the Church*, Vol. 6. Washington, D.C.: Catholic University of America Press, 1948.

Knox, R.A. *Enthusiasm.* New York: Oxford University Press, 1950, repr. 1961.

Lindblom, J. *Prophecy in Ancient Israel.* Philadelphia: Fortress Press, 1962.

McGuire, Meredith B. *The Social Context of Prophecy: "Word Gifts" of the Spirit among Catholic Pentecostals* in *Review of Religious Research*, Vol. 18, No. 2, Winter, 1977.

Nichol, John Thomas. *Pentecostalism.* New York: Harper & Row, 1966.

O'Connor, Edward D. *The Pentecostal Movement in the Catholic Church.* Notre Dame, Ind.: Ave Maria Press, 1971.

Rahner, Karl. *Sacramentum Mundi*, Vol. 1. New York: Herder & Herder, 1968.

Rowley, H.H., ed. *Studies in O.T. Prophecy.* New York: Charles Scribner's Sons, 1950.

Shepherd of Hermas in *The Fathers of the Church*, Vol. 1. Washington, D.C.: Catholic University of America Press, 1947.

Synave, P., and P. Benoit. *Prophecy and Inspiration.* Tr. by A. Dulles and T.L. Sheridan. New York: Desclée, 1961.

Tertullian. *On the Soul* in *The Fathers of the Church*, Vol. 10. Washington, D.C.: Catholic University of America Press, 1950.

Volken, L. *Visions, Revelations and the Church.* Tr. by E. Gallagher. New York: P.J. Kenedy, 1963.

Yocum, Bruce. *Prophecy*, Ann Arbor, Mich.: Servant Publications, 1976.